THE SIMPLE SCIENCE OF
WINE AND BEER MAKING

THE SIMPLE SCIENCE OF WINE AND BEER MAKING

H. E. BRAVERY

MACDONALD · LONDON

SBN 356 02646 9
First published in 1969 by
Macdonald & Co. (Publishers) Ltd.,
St. Giles House, 49 Poland Street, London, W.1.
Made and printed in Great Britain by
W. & G. Baird Ltd., Belfast

Contents

Author's Note   7

What a Recipe Amounts To   11

Fermentation   17

The Fermentation Lock   31

Spoilage   37

Utensils and Apparatus   43

Sterilizing   50

Using the Hydrometer   54

Enzyme Action in Beer-Making   71

Correcting Faults and Blending   83

Racking, 'Off' Flavours, and Clarifying Problems   92

Siphoning   105

Fermentation Cupboard   109

Sticking Ferments   112

Balance of Acid   116

Maturing, Storage Problems and Preserving   123

A Selection of Recipes   142

The Drake Trial Tube   165

Appendix   167

Author's Note

I have written elsewhere that I am an advocate of simpler methods. Indeed, I can see no reason at all why most wine- and beer-makers should not continue to use easy, straightforward recipes and methods for all their wines and beers once they have found those that suit them best.

This book is not intended to lure you from your chosen course or to try to influence you in using expensive equipment and apparatus. My aim has been to give the wine- and beer-maker a deeper understanding of the subject than I have been able to give in my simpler works, which concern themselves mainly with recipes and methods. In my previous books I was able only to touch upon the more technical aspects in order to give full recipes and methods for readers to work with. The decision to work on those lines proved to be the correct one. My simpler works have sold between them over 250,000 copies throughout the world and continue to sell at the rate of 4,000 to 5,000 copies a year each.

The idea of preparing a somewhat more technical work has not been wholly my own. Readers of my simpler books and my magazine articles and members of wine- and beer-making circles and clubs to which I give talks have been trying to persuade me to do this for some time. Their argument was, and evidently still is, that while they have learnt a lot from my earlier books, they would like to know a little more about the scientific aspects of the subject.

As one member of a wine-making circle put it: 'We have read the very technical books on the science and chemistry of wine- and beer-making, and most of us cannot make head or tail of them. We simply do not have the basic knowledge of chemistry needed to understand them. We have read your books and make good wines with them. What we want now is a book that goes further than any of yours do at present, but not nearly as far as the truly technical works which are, after all, intended mainly for the chemist or aspiring chemist.' This same person went on: 'What most of us are looking for is what might be called "The Simpler Science and Chemistry of Wine- and Beer-making".' Readers will now appreciate where I obtained not only the inspiration to prepare this book but also a most suitable title for it. The main problem was how far to go. I had to give the details asked for but at the same time keep them simple and explain the more technical aspects in a manner that everybody could understand. This, I think, I have managed to do.

But that was not the only problem. As most wine-makers know, the process, from the very moment when the fruits are gathered to the time when the wine is bottled and labelled, is a continuous one. But to write one long chapter from the beginning of the book to the end would not have made sense. I have therefore divided the process into various parts and written about each one separately. But because the process is continuous, every part is interrelated.

For this reason there is some inevitable repetition, for which I must ask your forgiveness. For example, when writing about fermentation, the subject of spoilage ferments was bound to crop up. Therefore, both topics are mentioned in the separate chapters covering each one. Knowing my readers as I do, I am sure they will not hold this against me.

As I mentioned before, this book is not intended to lure you from using simple recipes and methods. If it were, they would not be included. The main purpose is to provide you with background knowledge which will enable you to understand what goes on while wines and beers are making themselves. With this knowledge you are in a far better position to formulate your own ideas, evolve recipes if you want to, or do almost anything you please with any kind of ingredient. The book shows how you are able to make various types of wines by using the hydrometer and how you can get used to it.

All in all, this book is designed to take the home wine- and beer-maker as deeply into the subject as he need ever go and provide him with as much background knowledge of these subjects as he will ever require.

H. E. Bravery.

What a Recipe amounts to

A recipe is basically little more than a set of instructions to be followed under normal circumstances. There are good recipes and there are useless ones. But good or useless, a very great deal depends on the method used. A good recipe will make poor wine if it is used with an unsuitable method, while a poor recipe will make poor wine no matter what sort of method is used. Obviously, then, we want a good recipe with the most reliable and suitable method if we are to expect good results.

Wine-making is rather like driving a car or, for that matter, doing anything that calls for a bit of common sense. When learning to drive, you use someone else's recipe for driving. But when you have passed your test, you set about driving in your own way, bearing in mind what the instructor has instilled into you. If he was a good instructor, you will never forget the main essentials of driving because they will be instilled into you in the way that discipline is drilled into army recruits by a sergeant major.

And so it is with wine-making. You learn by the recipes of others and by your own mistakes. But what you learn on the way are the hard lessons that have to be learnt in anything that is worth doing well. If there has ever been a subject worth learning it is wine-making, both for the results themselves and for the fascinating hobby that goes with them.

The technical information found in this book is included for use not so much in the practical sense, but rather as background knowledge.

To revert for a moment to learning to drive. When you have done this, if you learn how everything works and how each working part relies upon the next for efficient performance, you automatically know what you can do with the car and how it will respond to your driving. You will also know instantly if something is not working properly.

And so it is with making wines and beers. Learn about the technical background, understand the basic principles, and you will be a far better wine- or beer-maker than if you follow recipes blindly without really understanding the whys and wherefores.

As you will see, a great deal goes on behind the scenes. There are a great many types and varieties of wines and beers, and it is for you to choose which one you want to make. The following recipes will take you near your goal. But when you have read and re-read this book, you will have such a clear understanding of precisely what goes on behind the scenes that you will be able to look at wine- and beer-making in a different light. You will be able to vary recipes or dispense with them altogether and forge ahead confidently with success assured.

No matter how much they may learn about these subjects, countless thousands will be content to follow recipes for evermore, and certainly no-one can blame them for that. But they will twist them here, turn them there, add a little more of 'this' or reduce 'that' by a little, and so on until they have made the initial recipe into what they wanted in the first place. Background knowledge of the subject will enable them to do this quite easily; without it, they would be completely stumped.

There is no need to alter or to try to balance any of the recipes in this book when using them for the first time, because they have been balanced already, in so far as they can be. Also you do not have to use any equipment other than normal utensils for making wines or beers. My recipes make wines and beers as I like them and as a lot of other people like them. I am sure that you will like them too. But if you want a slight variation, wait until you have read and understood the technical details of this book and made wines or beers with the recipes, then you will know what to do.

Almost all modern recipes – that is, those published since 1957 – are reliable. Those published before produced wines that suited people's tasks at the time. But during the last decade a new kind of wine-maker has emerged. No longer is he content to make the country wines of our grandmother's day which were often unpalatable concoctions. Travelling abroad has been instrumental in bringing about this change. People want wines like those of Continental countries and set about finding how to make them. Suppliers of ingredients, quick to notice this trend, put on the market the means of making such wines. Today, with simple recipes and sound background knowledge, there is hardly a Continental wine that we cannot imitate.

It is a fact that the main cause of disappointment with initial efforts is that amateurs do not give sufficient thought to the type of wine they are to make.

I have come across this so many times that I wonder how so many could be so stupid. Usually this happens when a neighbour or friend hands over surplus fruit so that the recipient makes wine with it. It could be apples, rhubarb, raspberries or, for that matter, any fruit you can think of. The results, although they may be first-class wines raved over by many, may disappoint the maker simply because, without realising it, he does not like this type of wine. The same applies to commercial wines. Each person has his own preference.

A balanced recipe contains a list of all the ingredients necessary for a fully flavoured and, as far as is possible, a chemically balanced wine. It is imperative that the must we prepare contains all the essential elements for successful fermentation. In preparing a must we simulate, in so far as we can, the chemical composition of grape juice. We do this because grape juice contains all these essential elements in the right proportions or near-right proportions for successful fermentation.

This is the reason why we add acid and tannin to musts prepared from ingredients that do not contain them; such as roots, flowers and certain dried fruits. If we do not make up these deficiencies, fermentation would be unsatisfactory in many ways, and the wine would not be worth tasting, let alone drinking.

This is also the reason why we use so little wild and garden fruits when we make wines with them. Usually they contain so much acid that, if we made wines with the undiluted juice, we would not be able to drink them owing to the high acidity and in some cases astringency. So we take the simple

way out by using what we consider to be the
amount of fruit that will put into the must the
amount of tannin and acid needed both for a good
fermentation and a reasonably well-balanced wine.

The amount of fruit used is usually between
three and six pounds depending on the type of wine
– light, heavy, dry, sweet – required. But here is
where a recipe can mislead.

During a normal to good season when fruits ripen
well, the acidity is lessened and sugar content increased, and a good recipe will turn out good wines.
But in a poor season when there has been a lot of
rain and very little sunshine, the sugar content of
the fruit will be very low and the acid content will
be high. The wine produced will be totally different
– apart from basic flavour – from the wine made in
a good season, even though the same fruit and recipe are used. It is in such cases that background
knowledge is so important for it enables you to
make allowances for the differences in sugar and
acid contents from season to season.

Other factors must also be taken into consideration, for example, soil conditions. Sand, clay and
chalk all make a difference to the fruits in one way
or another. Recipes cannot allow for this sort of
thing. If you gather fruits from the same area every
season there should be more consistency in their
chemical balance than if they are gathered from
widely differing places where each has been grown
on different soils. There should be very little in-
consistency in well-cultivated fruits from the same
garden. But even here, you must allow for the un-
reliability of our climate. Anybody liking a particular type of wine made from wild or garden fruits

would do well to cultivate these fruits in sufficient quantities for wine-making purposes.

You will now understand why you have been disappointed at odd times when using the same fruits with the same recipe.

Fermentation

This is the process which turns our musts into wine. Without fermentation, musts would remain more or less as we prepared them, for a short time at least. If we did not add suitable yeast, but merely left the prepared mixture to itself, fermentation of sorts would commence. And, undoubtedly, this would be caused by a mixture of undesirable yeasts and bacteria which were on the fruits when we prepared the must or which came into contact with it later. This aspect is covered more fully under the heading 'Spoilage', p. 37.

An enormous amount of study and research has been and still is being done on the process of fermentation. A century ago, it was barely understood; indeed, yeast was not generally accepted as the medium which brought about fermentation. Today, we could not hope to make wines without special yeast. By this I do not mean expensive yeast but selected yeast. There are countless varieties of yeast as we see under 'Spoilage', but the yeasts we use to make wines must be pure. They must not be contaminated with wild, or undesirable yeast. Every possible care is taken to ensure that the yeasts we buy are suitable for our purpose and as pure as modern processes will allow.

Yeast, it may surprise many, is a living thing. When obtained it is inactive, or dormant. It is classed as a fungus because it must live on other matter instead of providing food for itself as plants do through their leaves and stems.

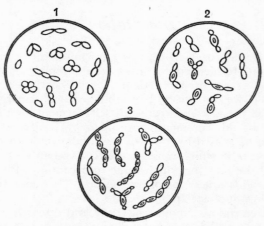

Yeast under Microscope
The illustration shows how the yeast cells multiply

Therefore, to produce wines from the musts we prepare we add yeast of a special type and give it the means not only to become active, but also to live and reproduce itself. In return, it produces a number of by-products, the main one being alcohol. In addition, glycerine, acetaldehyde, and other substances are produced in quite minute quantities. Yet these are important to the fullness or completeness of fermentation.

It has been found that enzymes (see p. 77) secreted by the yeast cells bring about the all-important changes necessary for full and complete fermentation. It seems that yeast, given suitable conditions, will produce the enzymes that it needs to take itself through all the necessary stages of fermentation. As one enzyme completes its work, it stops (becomes inactive) to allow another to take over. If this were not the case, too much of certain substances, and not enough of others, would be produced. But this does not happen.

All in all, yeast and the enzymes it produces form a complex system complete in itself, relying only on the means of sustaining itself. And this it does on the sugar we put into the must. But if we give it too much sugar to begin with its reaction is slow and erratic, or perhaps it will not react at all. Hence the general desirability of starting our ferments at a specific gravity of not more than 1·110. Hence also the need to produce in the must a certain amount of acid, tannin and other desirable matter.

As already mentioned, yeast is dormant when purchased. If we add it to the must in this state, we may have to wait several days for it to become active. So we make what we call a nucleus ferment. In doing this we produce a colony of active yeasts which, when put into a prepared must, will start the must into active fermentation almost immediately. The overriding importance of this is that the prepared must is not left open for a day or so to attacks by wild yeasts and bacteria. Even when covered as directed in the methods, a must where there is no fermentation going on is open to attack because there is not a constant stream of carbon dioxide gas (CO_2) escaping through the puckers of the tied-down covering to keep out the air.

This brings me to the importance of what we call fermenting under *anaerobic conditions* – fermenting

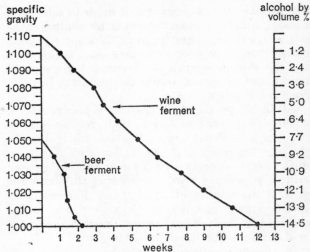

Fermentation Chart No. 1

We see that the hydrometer readings on the left of the chart are in the reverse of their order on the hydrometer itself. This has been arranged so that we may see how, as sugar is used up, the readings drop and the alcohol content increases.

in the absence of atmospheric oxygen. Years ago, at the age of five, I was introduced to home-made wines by falling head first into a tub of fermenting dandelions in my grandfather's outhouse. And, alas, until recently open fermentation was still practised. Yeast creates anaerobic conditions for itself to a certain degree, but it cannot prevent the escape of the gas it produces. By covering fermenting wines with tied-down sheet polythene, we can control the release of the gas and leave the wine fermenting with a protective cloud of carbon dioxide gas above it.

Later, we put the fermenting wines under fermentation locks (see p. 33), usually at the stage where the fermentation has slowed down and where the gas being produced would no longer be sufficient to form a protective cloud.

From all this it will be seen at once that yeast produces not only all the essentials for a full and complete fermentation, but also its own protection from wild yeasts and bacteria in so far as it can. When the yeast leaves off, we take over in order to safeguard it and the wine we are preparing.

But whatever happens during the fermentation, most amateurs are concerned mainly in the production of alcohol, flavours, and bouquet.

When using English wild and garden fruits we cannot use enough to produce in a must the amount of sugar needed to make the amount of alcohol we want, simply because these fruits contain too much acid and would produce wine that would be too astringent. For example, we might need as much as thirty pounds of blackberries or elderberries or even sixty pounds of plums or damsons to produce a gallon of wine, depending on the amount of juice in the fruits in a particular season.

So when we use, say, four to six pounds of fruit to the gallon in order to obtain as near as possible the strength of flavour we need – not forgetting roughly the amount of acid we need as well – there is a grave shortage of sugar. Obviously, with so little fruit being used, the amount of fruit sugar in a must will be very small, enough perhaps to make about 2% of alcohol. And since good wines require alcohol in the region of 14% by volume, we must obviously add sugar according to the type of wine we want and the amount of alcohol we want it to contain.

Here it is important to understand the meaning of alcohol tolerance of yeasts. In general, we use the word 'tolerate' to mean the limit of our endurance or 'the amount we can put up with'. So we can call the maximum tolerance of yeast 'the amount of alcohol it can put up with'. And this is in the region of 14 or 15% by volume. When this level is reached, the yeast is destroyed by the alcohol, no more fermentation takes place, and no more alcohol is made.

When yeast is added to a must, its first action is to convert the household sugar we add to 'invert sugar'. This is brought by an enzyme in the yeast known as invertase. This change is necessary because yeast cannot ferment cane sugar in the form in which it is usually added. Having done this, the yeast almost at once begins to reproduce itself. Each yeast cell – so tiny that something like three thousand of them could queue across a halfpenny – sends out a bud which in turn sends out another bud, and so on. At certain stages the cell looks something like a deformed potato. (See 'Yeast under Microscope', p. 18.)

During this reproduction process the yeast feeds upon the sugar, turning approximately half into alcohol and half into carbon dioxide gas. It is in the early stages of yeast reproduction, that fermentation is very vigorous and the production of alcohol is quite high. The colony of yeast continues to reproduce millions of new cells as others die. Initially the production of new yeasts exceeds the death of others, so that we have an increasing number of yeast cells hour by hour.

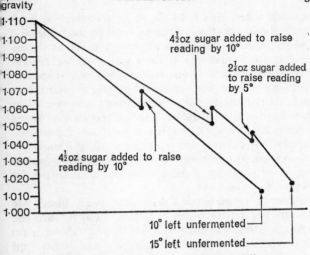

Fermentation Chart No. 2   For Sweet Wines

In this example we see the effect of starting with a specific
gravity of 1·110 and adding sugar during fermentation. In
one we have added 4½ oz to raise the reading 10°, and in the
other we have added 4½ oz plus 2¼ oz to raise reading to a
total of 15°.

In both cases we are left with the added sugar registering on
the hydrometer as unfermented.

This is precisely what we wanted, because we began with a
specific gravity of 1·110 to make the alcohol we wanted and
added sugar so that when the alcohol had been made, we
were left with the added sugar in the wine to sweeten it.

In both cases we achieved the intended drop of 1·110 and
made the amount of alcohol corresponding to this drop —
14·5% by volume.

After a while, the rate slows down, and it is at this
stage that those who evolve methods and recipes, as
I do myself, recommend putting the wine under
fermentation locks (see p. 31). We judge as near as

possible when this is likely to be necessary and include the instruction in the method in the hope that
the individual operator's must will react as we expect it to. Sometimes it does not, and we receive
indignant letters from readers whose wines are
climbing out of the jars through the fermentation
lock. Fortunately, these happenings are rare. The
slowing down of fermentation is increased by using
a fermentation lock because we cut off the oxygen
supply. This causes the yeast to turn to the sugar for
its oxygen, thus using up more sugar and producing a little more alcohol that if it obtained its
oxygen from outside.

After a fermentation lock has been fitted, we
usually regard the wine as having stepped into the
secondary fermentation stage, although there is no
clear distinction between the primary (first) and
secondary stages because the two overlap. By
secondary, we mean, in general, the less vigorous
fermentation that goes on perhaps for several
months according to the compositions of the must,
temperature, and other factors which have bearing
on the length of fermentation.

Composition of the Must

A reasonably well-balanced must made up from a
good recipe will contain all the essentials for full
and complete fermentation. Until a few years ago,
hardly any amateur had heard of yeast nutrients
which we now add in order to help the yeast to make
the maximum alcohol.

I have said that yeast and the enzymes it produces
form a complex system capable of producing its own
needs to take it through fermentation. This is true

as regards the enzymes needed for this purpose. But yeast needs more than that to give it the basis from which to work. The yeast can reproduce itself on sugar alone, but if it is to continue to do this and survive the strength of alcohol it produces it must have other things as well. If it does not get them, fermentation is likely to stop early on so that perhaps only 8 or 9% of alcohol by volume or less is made. (See 'Sticking Ferments', p. 112.)

English wild and garden fruits undoubtedly contain most of the essential needs of the yeast. But bear in mind that we dilute these juices to such an extent that these essentials are reduced practically to insignificance, in the same way as the sugar they contain. To make up for this dilution we add the essential substances in the form of chemical *nutrients,* just as we add sugar.

Some very wild claims are made for certain commercially produced nutrients, so treat them with reserve. A good nutrient will contain a balanced consortium of all the chemicals the yeast is likely to need and certainly those in which our greatly diluted musts are deficient. Several important chemicals will be found in sufficient quantity even in greatly diluted musts. But generally we must add ammonium sulphate, magnesium sulphate (Epsom salts) and potassium phosphate. All of these, with certain additives, are contained in a good nutrient.

There is no doubt that these chemicals assist enzyme action. Indeed, it is wise to add a good nutrient at the start of fermentation or prior to adding the yeast and more later in the process, preferably before fermentation slows down to any appreciable extent.

Temperature

This is another important factor affecting fermentation. And although some writers on the subject recommend a figure as high as 80°F, I have found that a reasonably constant temperature in the region of 65° to 70°F during the initial fermentation is perfectly satisfactory.

Making wines all the year round is quite simple these days. But it used to be almost impossible in the old days. Wines made in late summer or early autumn almost always stopped fermenting on the first cold night of late autumn or early winter. This resulted in the wine-maker thinking that his wine had ceased altogether. And so he bunged it down to clear and, when ready, bottled it as a finished product. When a warm spell, in February or perhaps a bit later, penetrated to the yeast, it became active again and began to make the amount of alcohol it would have made if the cold had not prevented it.

This meant that corks or bungs flew out, and the wine clouded as yeast was brought into suspension by the agitation of renewed fermentation. Many wine-makers thought their wines had gone wrong and threw them away. Others did go wrong because the blown bungs were not noticed and the wines were left uncovered and therefore open to attacks by wild yeasts and bacteria. This is covered more fully under 'Spoilage', p. 37.

Today, all these troubles are a thing of the past because we can use thermostatically controlled heaters to keep our wines at the correct temperature. They can be installed quite cheaply and are inexpensive to run. (See 'Fermentation Cupboard',

p. 109.) This enables fermentation to go on un-
hindered throughout the coldest weather and ensures trouble-free wine-making with the maximum
alcohol being made without undue problems.

Trouble-free continuous fermentation is of the
utmost importance for top-quality results; flavour,
bouquet, and all-round quality depends on this.

Preparing a Nucleus

As mentioned, we rarely add yeast in its dormant
state because of the delay before it becomes active.
In preparing a nucleus in the following manner, we
are able to have a small batch of yeast already fermenting to add to a prepared must. I am aware, of
course, that a great many people use yeast successfully without preparing a nucleus, but there will
always be those who confound the critics.

Many proprietory yeasts are supplied with directions for making a nucleus, but there are no hard
and fast rules except that it should be reasonably
balanced. By this, I do not mean that each little part
of it must be measured. What I mean is that we
should use a fruit juice, which, for all intents and
purposes, may be regarded as balanced when diluted
with a little water and sugar. Lemon, orange, or any
other fruit juice or diluted fruit syrups such as
Ribena are all perfectly satisfactory. Even diluted
malt extract is suitable. But if we use this, we must
add a little acid and tannin as well.

You can make a good nucleus with 1 fl oz of any
fruit juice and 5 fl oz of water in which 2 oz of sugar
have been boiled. If the juice is lemon or orange,
add a tablespoon of strong tea as well to make up
for the deficiency of tannin in the citrus fruits. Add

the yeast to the liquid and pour it into a small, narrow-necked bottle. Plug the neck with a firm knob of cotton wool to protect it against the ingress of wild yeast and bacteria.

In a few days, the nucleus is fermenting enough to be put into the must as an already active colony of yeast. Before removing the cotton wool from the bottle, run a lighted match round the wool just enough to scorch it lightly. By doing this you destroy any yeast or bacteria collected there ready to drop in when the cotton wool is removed. Shake the bottle and put most of the nucleus into the must.

After you have done this, replenish the nucleus with more of the original material. In this way, you can keep the yeast alive ready for the next must. There is no need to add more yeast because the little remaining will breed more yeast for you. You will, in fact, be breeding your own supplies of yeast.

It will readily be seen that by adding a colony of active yeast to the must, there is no long pause between adding the yeast and fermentation as there would be if dormant yeast were added. This obviously cuts to a minimum the risk of bacterial infection.

Fermentation is seen as frothing on the surface of the must and a gentle hissing or fizzing which is quite audible. There is also a smell quite different from that of the fruits being fermented.

During the first few days, fermentation is usually very vigorous, the wine becoming warmed by energy produced by the yeast. Furthermore, where fruits are being fermented, the pips and skins rise to form a cake upon the surface. For this reason it is wise to allow several inches of headroom in the fermenting vessel. When juices only are fermented, a heavy frothing will appear.

The secondary fermentation stage is often regarded as imminent when the cake of skins levels off to flatness and when the froth of a juice ferment peters out, leaving the surface reasonably free from froth. When the heavier part of the cake of skins has sunk and the frothing of a juice ferment has completely stopped, it is reasonable to assume that the secondary fermentation has begun.

It is at this stage, regardless of directions to the contrary in methods, that the fruits should be pressed free of juice and the wine strained into a jar to be put under a fermentation lock. Juice ferments are treated similarly but need no straining. During the stage under fermentation locks, fermentation continues slowly but surely and the amount of alcohol increases accordingly.

Do not be worried by prolonged fermentation. Indeed, a long, steady fermentation is of great importance in producing good-quality wines.

The fermentation lock is a good guide to the progress of fermentation, and it is safe to say that all the time the solution in the lock is pushed up to the outgoing side, a little fermentation is still going on regardless of whether bubbles are passing through or not. It must be borne in mind that the longer fermentation continues, the more alcohol there is produced and that this alcohol is having a weakening effect upon the yeast. This effect continues until the maximum amount of alcohol the yeast can tolerate is finally reached. At this stage the whole complex yeast system is destroyed, and, as we have seen, fermentation ceases. The last of the minute solids forming slight hazes in the wine settle out now that there is no longer any disturbance caused by yeast action to keep them in suspension.

Many people tend to become worried by a slow fermentation and either increase the temperature or lower it in the hope of creating more favourable conditions for the yeast. Both these courses are unwise. First, over-heating can destroy the yeast and harm the must. Secondly, lowering the temperature to any great extent can cause the yeast to go dormant.

In both cases, re-starting the yeast may be very difficult and attempts are often quite futile. Even adding new yeast or some of the original nucleus may fail simply because the percentage of alcohol present comes as a too great a shock to the yeast. Bear in mind that there is no alcohol present when the yeast is normally added to a must and that, during the course of fermentation, the yeast becomes accustomed to an ever-increasing amount of alcohol. But putting yeast into a must already containing, say, 10–11% of alcohol, is a very different matter.

The Fermentation Lock

There is no doubt that this little piece of equipment is one of the most important in the wine-maker's armoury, and it is a pity that certain writers on this subject tend to lead people to think otherwise.

When the wine is racked for the first time and is then put into jars, fermentation locks are fitted as a matter of course. Sterilizing solution is poured in to the level shown and fermentation is allowed to proceed under anaerobic conditions. This state is, as discussed under 'Fermentation', created by the yeast itself by the production of a heavier-than-air cloud of carbon dioxide gas above the wine. A thin tube of glass stuffed with cotton wool would allow the excess gas to escape and would prevent the ingress of bacteria, insects and moulds which cause the wines to spoil.

If this were all that is needed, then fermentation locks could be dispensed with. But this is not so. Bear in mind that fermentation locks are used during what we call the secondary fermentation stage and, as we have seen, this is the stage where fermentation gradually slows down. It is during the slowing down that some sort of trap is necessary to retain sufficient gas and at the same time release the excess. This function is performed admirably by the sterilizing solution in the fermentation lock.

Water would suffice for this purpose were it not

for some special considerations. First, water cannot remain pure indefinitely, and any moulds or bacteria that might come into contact with it would automatically contaminate it. Indeed, I have seen wine flies actually drown themselves in the water in the lock in their desperate efforts to reach the wine under its protection.

During the quite vigorous ferment that usually goes on for a few days after the lock is fitted, the see-saw action of the water could mean that a tiny amount might be thrown far back and find its way down the stem of the lock and into the jar. And if this water were already contaminated, the wine might well be affected. So using sterilizing solution is the best plan, for any bacteria or moulds are destroyed by it.

Further, it sometimes happens that the pressure in the jar falls owing to sudden cold contracting the wine, and air is drawn into the jar. The air is purified because it has to pass through the sterilizing solution. The lock is in fact working in reverse. This occurrence is nothing to worry about, but it does tend to puzzle newcomers.

Apart from the advantages already described, the fermentation lock is a very good guide to the rate of fermentation. This is indicated by the rate at which bubbles are seen passing through. Early on, they may form an almost continuous stream, but later fermentation slows down and bubbles are observed only at long intervals. Later still, there may be no evidence that fermentation is continuing except for the solution being pushed up on the out-going side of the lock. A gas bubble might pass through at intervals of every one or two hours, but because no-

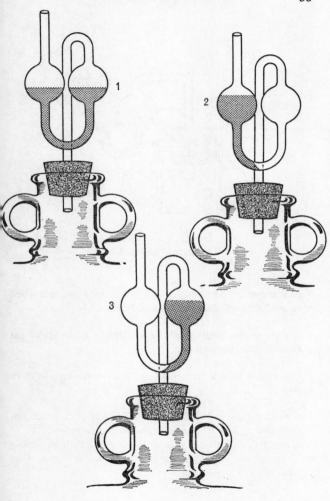

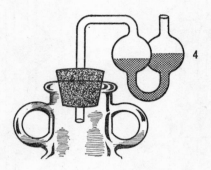

The Fermentation Lock

Fig. 1 shows a fermentation lock fitted to a jar and filled with sterilising solution to the usual level.

Fig. 2 shows the position of the solution as a bubble of gas is about to pass through it.

Fig. 3 shows how a fermentation lock sometimes works in reverse.

Fig. 4. This type of lock is very useful where little headroom is available, such as in a small fermentation cupboard.
The one drawback of this type is that, because little sterilising solution can be put in, frequent topping-up is necessary to prevent the lock drying out.

one can watch it for this long there appears to be no activity at all. It is therefore sound practice to leave the wine under the lock all the time the solution is pushed up.

Later, it will be observed that after a long, slow fermentation lasting several months, the solution is drawn up the wrong side. The lock should be examined daily after this in order to note when the solution has returned to normal – that is, when all the solution remains at the bottom of the U-bend. When this state is observed, it is safe to say that fermentation has ceased.

Users of the hydrometer will know for sure by taking the reading to ascertain whether or not the maximum alcohol for the type of wine being made has been reached. Those not using the hydrometer are advised to leave the wine under locks and in a warm place for three or four weeks before regarding it safe to rack and set aside for storing. This is advised for the very simple reason that, although the lock indicates that fermentation has ceased, there can still be a few yeast spores not yet killed that can carry on the fermentation for a few days longer.

When using the type of fermentation lock illustrated it is advisable to insert a small plug of cotton wool in the open end in order to give double protection to the wine. The solution, which will slowly lose its strength, should be replenished from time to time. There is no need to remove the lock for this, merely add a few drops with an eye-dropper or pipette.

Glass locks are often difficult to insert and remove from bungs. To ease this situation, merely moisten the stem with water or sterilizing solution.

Rubber bungs take a mighty grip on the stem of locks that have been in jars for months on end. Twisting to remove the locks will break the fragile glass. To break the grip, immerse lock and bung in water for a few minutes. The bung will then slide off easily.

Spoilage

When you realize the number of troubles that can beset the wine-maker, you might well ask how on earth he ever manages to make good wines. The simple answer is that he has come to realize that prevention of trouble is better than attempts to cure the result, and he works accordingly. Therefore he has no trouble.

But there are people making wines who often have them turn to vinegar; go insipid and flat; take on odours that have nothing to do with the decomposition of vegetable matter and dead yeast cells; become sharp or apparently over-acid on storage; have medicinal flavours; become thick and oily; become harsh of flavour and assume an overpowering or sickly bouquet; or become sickly sweet to the palate. All these troubles, besides a few that are peculiar to individual wine-makers, are quite easily avoided. But without understanding the causes, no-one would know the preventive measures that are necessary.

Most modern methods in circulation include the necessary precautions but, unfortunately, many pre-1958 publications are still used, and countless recipes and methods from our grandparents' day are still in circulation. Indeed, even in these enlightened times, a few magazines still pump out these antiquities. Their editors, always on the look-out for simple methods for their readers, refuse to

believe that modern methods can turn out wines
superior to many with long names and expensive
pedigrees from the Continent. So the poor reader
has little chance of success. Anybody, with the right
kind of recipe, using the right method, and having
a little background knowledge can turn out wines
comparable with those from almost any country you
care to name. And almost the whole of the secret of
success lies in preventing wines from being spoiled.

Any method that calls for gathering the fruits and
then letting them ferment without added yeast
should be put on the fire at once. And so should
any that do not call for sterilizing the fruit either
by boiling or by using sulphite (Campden tablets),
whether added yeast is recommended or not. This is
because the gathered fruits already have yeasts in
them. Some of them may be quite useful, but with
them almost invariably come many wild (unculti-
vated) spoilage yeasts.

In addition to the wild yeasts, several species of
bacteria and moulds are also present. If the must is
not sterilized by one means or another, any of these
can set up a fermentation of sorts alongside the fermentation brought about by the desirable yeast so
that any of the troubles mentioned above can occur
very readily.

Acetification, or wine turning to vinegar, is one
of the most common troubles. Although it is possible to halt this disease in its stride if detected very
early, it is rare that the trouble is discovered until
irreparable damage has been done. Acetification is
caused by the vinegar bacteria *mycoderma aceti*.
Having gained access to the wine or having been
present on damaged fruit, the bacteria convert the

alcohol produced into acetic acid which is the main constituent of vinegar.

Lactic acid bacteria, of which there are many species, are the cause of many troubles, including ropiness or oiliness. Wines afflicted with this disease take on an oily appearance and may indeed pour like oil. The flavour is impaired, but not to a great extent. However, the condition and the appearance of the wine make it quite unpalatable.

You can cure this trouble by dissolving $1\frac{1}{2}$ to 2 Campden tablets in each gallon of wine and stirring it vigorously for several minutes. If you leave the wine for some time, deposit settles out in a similar way to an ordinary deposit, but this one is usually of loose consistency and is easily disturbed. Some people seem content to drink a wine revived in this fashion, but to my mind the disease and the drastic treatment it requires renders a wine not worth having.

Sweet to semi-sweet wines are sometimes attacked by a species of lactic bacteria which feeds upon the sugar to produce a number of by-products which impart peculiar off-flavour, bitterness, or a very difficult to describe sickly sweetness to the wine.

This is not the same as an over-sweet wine; the sweetness appears in after-taste rather than on the tongue. Often with these wines, there are also other flavours which cannot be described because there are so many of them. And a most surprising fact is that I have had this sort of affected wine offered me at various places (no names, no pack drill) by people who simply could not detect their presence. Obviously, the disease was in its early stages, but within a few days the wine would be irretrievably lost.

Finished dry wines are not affected by lactic bacteria because of the absence of sugar. But careless production could allow the trouble to run alongside fermentation before all the sugar is used up.

In certain cases wines affected by lactic acid bacteria appear to take on a silky sheen, the density of which depends on the extent to which the disease has progressed—and this depends on the amount of sugar either attacked during fermentation or the amount of sugar left in the wine and attacked at a later stage.

Mild attacks are not easily distinguishable, but moderate to severe attacks can be seen as a silky sheen in the wine. While the disease can be cured, the effects in taste and bouquet of the wine cannot, so the only remedy for such wine is to get rid of it and thoroughly sterilize all utensils and corks that have come into contact with it.

Flowers of wine is another affliction. This is seen as tiny white flecks of mould on the surface. These gradually enlarge and join up so that the wine appears to have grown a carpet of felt. This disease is caused by mould yeast and film yeasts which attack the alcohol, converting it to carbon dioxide and water.

A cure for flowers of wine, if taken in the early stage, is to insert a tube with a funnel attached into the wine and pour similar wine into the funnel. The end of the tube should be mid-way down the jar. As the jar fills up and overflows, the mould-like flecks get expelled from the jar. Treatment thereafter is the same as that recommended for ropiness. After treatment the wine should be allowed time to clarify, when it should be siphoned off from any deposit and used as soon as possible, because it is likely that further attacks may occur in a wine once it has been affected.

There are other causes of spoiled wines which have nothing to do with bacteria or undesirable yeasts. These come in various forms from using unsuitable utensils. Bear in mind that many utensils are quite dangerous. Those old crocks so fashionable 20 years ago and, alas, still in use in many areas, are often lead-glazed. Reaction of fruit acids on the lead can produce wines capable of giving their maker lead poisoning. Indeed, this has happened many, many times. The cumulative effect of this is fatal.

The difference between salt-glaze, which is quite safe, and lead-glaze is usually distinguishable only by an expert. So do use modern utensils that can be trusted. In any case, a lead-glazed vessel might have hairline cracks that go unnoticed or small patches where the glaze is so thin that porous patches of clay show through. All these are hideouts for bacteria, which are unlikely to be destroyed by a quick rinse with sterilizing solution. If this sort of fault exists, then all precautions taken in other directions are wasted.

Copper, iron, zinc, and what are commonly known as galvanized vessels should be avoided like the plague. There is no need to use them today, although there was little else available 20 years ago. Metal contamination, as we call it, is responsible for *hazes* that appear in wines at later stages. They are rarely seen until the wine has been stored and then brought out for use. Ordinary clarifiers have little or no effect on these hazes, and you usually have to resort to filtering. This can very easily cause oxidation, or the absorption of too much oxygen.

Metals, in addition to causing hazes, impart disagreeable flavours – many wines do, indeed, take on a medicinal flavour. When drinking the wine, you may think that you are taking some sort of iron tonic instead. You can rid the wines of their hazes, but the flavours persist.

Utensils and Apparatus

As has been touched upon under 'Spoilage', p. 37, the choice of utensils is of far greater importance than is generally realized. Years ago, wine- and beer-makers were simply not catered for, so they *had* to use whatever they could lay their hands on. Very few of them realized that they were using utensils that caused spoilage in wines or that could turn out deadly poisonous wines.

Today, wine-makers have a wide choice of equipment. But we need not make it expensive – indeed, the initial outlay for making one- or two-gallon lots is quite small. Bear in mind that several two-gallon batches a year add up to a nice amount of wine. If, like many, you drink your wines soon after they are made, then five-gallon lots are more sensible. And, if you want to, you can make ten or twenty gallons at a time. It is sound advice, however, to make one- or two-gallon batches to start with until you really get the feel of things. The initial outlay for the smaller batches is also more attractive.

Metals must, of course, be used when water, fruits, or fruit juices are boiled. And they should be used for this purpose only. On no account should any metal be used for fermentation purposes. Also the fruits should be left in contact with metal for the shortest possible time. This is because fruit acids will attack any metal if they are in contact with it long enough. The result of this has been discussed under 'Spoilage'.

The most suitable metals to use for boiling water and for fruits or juices are monel metal, stainless steel, high-grade aluminium and, provided it is designed for cooking purposes, unchipped enamel. Enamel pails and similar utensils are not designed for cooking.

Fermentation should always be carried out in non-toxic polythene, glass, or new stoneware. Barrels are suitable, of course, provided that they are new or have been used for nothing except wine-making, and, they are easily cleaned and sterilized. One of the greatest mistakes (and one I have myself been forced to making owing to shortages years ago) is to use jars or barrels from other than a reliable dealer. How often has a wine-maker had an acquaintance tell him that he has heard that he makes wine and if he likes to collect them there are half a dozen old stone jars 'up the end of the garden'. And how many unsuspecting wine-makers have gone after them like a shot.

Thank heaven we know better today. Even so, almost every week letters reach me from readers of my other books and of my magazine articles asking my opinion of the usefulness of certain vessels they have been given. Amongst these are old vinegar barrels, barrels that have contained vegetable oils or fruit juices and the like. Others write that have acquired large plastic vessels of various shapes that have contained mild acids or other substances. Others confess that they have not the slightest idea what the vessels once contained.

In every case, for safety's sake I have advised

throwing them away. In the first case, it is impossible to get rid of the taste and smell of vinegar, so that any wine put into such a vessel would automatically acquire the taste of vinegar whether vinegar bacteria attacked the wine or not – which is more than likely – no matter how thorough attempts to clean might be.

Containers that have held fruit juices, syrups, or vegetable or cooking oils might be suitable if the nature of the plastic could be determined, and then cleaned so that they are safe. But as this is nigh-on impossible, it is best not to use them.

As for those that have contained acids of any sort, these should be destroyed. Many dangerous acids, some of which contain hydrochloric acid (spirits of salt) – a deadly poison – are now available in plastic containers. Whether these could be safely cleaned and whether the plastic itself is suitable for our purposes is doubtful.

The straight-from-the-shoulder advice must therefore be, obtain your supplies from reliable firms dealing in your requirements. A list of these appear at the end of the book.

Glass containers that have contained fruit cordials or the larger vessels of distilled water are quite safe as these are easily sterilized. So if you know of a cheap source of supply of such vessels, take advantage of it.

Dealers in home wine-making and brewing ingredients and utensils hold large supplies of the utensils most suitable for our needs. Since they know precisely the type of vessel and the materials they should be made from, it goes without saying that these are the best people to go to.

Many hardware stores supply plastic vessels that might be considered suitable, but the assistant might not be able to tell you precisely the type of plastic used in its manufacture, and this is important. Alcohol produced during fermentation may attack the plasticizers used in plasticized P.V.C. and similar vessels, so that the wine may become contaminated.

Polythene, P.V.C. (in which the plasticizer has not been used) Terylene, and nylon are quite suitable. But plastic vessels are not necessarily labelled as to what they are made of, and the assistant in the hardware stores will often sell you anything without knowing what you want it for. In any case, he would not know whether it was suitable or not. A wide range of sizes of all containers is available. All the wine-maker has to do is to decide in the light of the quantities he produces what size and type of vessel he needs.

A person setting out to make one-gallon lots will need a two-gallon polythene or other suitable plastic fermentation vessel, such as a pail, and a few one-gallon size glass or stoneware jars for the secondary fermentation and for storage. Vessels for boiling the fruits or juices (where this is done) or for boiling the water will most likely already be in his kitchen. So he will need very little, apart from straining cloths, funnels – which must be of suitable plastic – and fermentation locks. The more adventurous will need larger vessels of which there are plenty in the price lists of suppliers of home wine-making equipment.

There is no doubt that glass vessels are fast becoming the most popular for the secondary fermentation stage, and even for storage where red wines can be kept in the dark. Glass allows the operator to see what is going on.

For the home brewer, there are polythene dustbins for mashing and fermenting purposes. Being lightweight and unbreakable, they are very popular. Those making draught beers will have to use stone tap-hole jars for storage. They are rather expensive but need only be bought once. And you will need only two or three because they are emptied a week or two after being filled.

Large polythene seamless bags have made their appearance in recent years and have become quite popular. These of course must be supported by such things as a barrel past its usefulness or a fairly strong wooden box. But make sure first that there are no protruding nails or splinters, otherwise the bag will be punctured.

Although in my view it is almost an insult to wines to put them into vessels shaped like a jerry-can, there is no doubt that this type of plastic vessel is becoming increasingly popular for the secondary fermentation stage and for fermentation purposes. They are unbreakable, light, and easy to carry about.

So before you buy new utensils or replace old ones, have a good look through several price lists, or better still visit your nearest supplier, in order to see just what is available – you will be surprised, I am sure.

Measures

While on the subject of utensils, a word about measuring is timely. It is well worthwhile making sure that jugs or other vessels are graduated in pints, quarts, half-gallon and so on up to near the rim. Jugs are usually marked in quarter pints, half pints, and so on. Small measures for measuring fluid ounces are usually marked for teaspoon and table-spoon. And bear in mind that these are recognized measures. So do not use a teaspoon or tablespoon from the cutlery drawer because they are likely to be wide of the true measure. How often one reads in recipes of the need for a level teaspoonful or tablespoonful of such and such. Yet there are a dozen different sizes of teaspoons and tablespoons.

Therefore, use a proper measure and work more safely – especially when you are measuring acid or some constituent that will have a very marked effect upon the flavour of the wine.

Corking

Just let me say that I have never yet found the need to use a corking machine. This is because I always use the flanged (flat-topped, mushroom shaped) corks with a plastic seal. They are quite cheap and are best bought by the gross. They are slipped over the top of the cork at bottling time, pressed down all round and allowed to dry out. As they do so in an hour or so, they shrink to form an airtight seal and become very, very tight after a while. They are easily removed when the wine is required.

A word about storing these seals. They come in an airtight can filled with fluid. Once the can has been opened I like to turn the lot into a small kilner jar or other screw-top of about 1 lb size. Some 'instant' coffee jars are ideal. Bear in mind that the jar must be kept airtight, otherwise the fluid that keeps the seals expanded will evaporate, and the seals shrink and become useless.

I have covered all the essential equipment in this section. If you are pressed into buying non-essentials, your wine- and beer-making will become expensive. So get the bare essentials to start with, and you will see then that you have everything you need.

Sterilizing

There is no doubt that in the past – and in the present also where negligence is encountered – almost all spoilage of wines was caused by not sterilizing the initial must or utensils. Sterilizing the must is included in any good method, so there is no need to mention it here.

However, sterilization of the must is useless in preventing spoilage if we neglect to sterilize all the utensils, including bottles, corks, hydrometers and their flasks, fermenting vessels, jars, funnels, and so on. This is because the diseases which attack wines are everywhere, in the same way as those that attack humans.

Wine, like the human body, is very susceptible to attacks by bacteria. But, unlike the human body, wine has no natural means of combating attacks. In other words, there are no antibodies present in wines capable of fighting disease as there are in the human body. Every utensil used must be regarded as a likely source of infection by one of the many diseases of wines. They must be sterilized in a similar fashion to the instruments used for surgical operations on the human body.

Fortunately, this is a very simple matter, which fits into the general plan of wine-making without inconvenience of any sort. To be able to do this with a minimum of bother, and to have plenty of sterilizing solution always on hand in case unexpected bottling or racking become necessary at short notice, it is important to have a stock of sulphur dioxide solution. Sulphur dioxide is undoubtedly the most reliable means of sterilization and it is used by the trade. Indeed, cellars where wines are bottled are fumigated with sulphur.

Bear in mind that the many bacteria that cause disease in wine are in the air and therefore likely to be inside jars and bottles, on corks, and so on. And it is a fact that many people are careless in their wine-making to the extent that they actually attract the disease to their products. Fermenting musts left uncovered, small amounts of wine or lees left in bottles or jars, fruit pulps from the straining bag, and vessels put away without being cleaned of all traces of wine attract disease.

Put the pulp from a strained must outside the back door and, within a few minutes, there will be at least a dozen fruit flies buzzing around it. These are harmless in themselves, but they act as carriers for other diseases, especially the disease caused by acetic bacteria which convert alcohol to vinegar. For this reason, these flies are wrongly called 'vinegar flies.' Attract these flies near to the house and in minutes they will be inside if they smell wines. And if you happen to be performing some operation that necessitates exposing wines to the air for a little while, they will be after the wine like a shot.

The same applies to other bacteria. The spores of wild, or spoilage yeasts and moulds are always present and are often seen in colonies as white or grey patches on jams or cheeses left exposed, on jars of meat paste, and in dirty wine and beer bottles. This being the case, yeasts and moulds must also be present on utensils, corks, and so on. Though inactive, they are ready to become active as soon as a medium suitable for them comes into contact with the utensils. Wine, of course, is a very suitable medium. Destruction of all these likely causes of disease is clearly necessary if trouble is to be avoided.

Sulphur dioxide is a gas. We can produce it in aqueous solution, and therefore in a very convenient form to use, by dissolving metabisulphite crystals in water. Small amounts of solution may be produced in an emergency from Campden fruit-preserving tablets used for sterilizing fruit musts, but this methods is not suitable for use with a large amount of utensils or even for repeated use on small amounts. It is far better and cheaper to make a stock solution.

I find half a gallon of solution a very convenient amount, but a quart would be more suitable for many people. To make half a gallon, buy 4 oz of sodium or potassium metabisulphite crystals from a chemist. Do not accept this if it is lumpy as it is very difficult to break down. Dissolve the crystals in a quart of hot water, stirring with something non-metal, such as a wooden spoon, until all the crystals have dissolved. Then make up to half a gallon with cold water. To make a quart, halve the quantities.

Corked well, the solution will keep its potency for as long as six months. It has rather a suffocating smell. But the only means of testing it to see if it is still strong enough after long storage and repeated use is to smell it. Do not take a powerful sniff at close quarters or at the neck of the jar. Approach it carefully, taking repeated sniffs as you get closer.

All the time there is a strong smell of sulphur, the solution is suitable for use. Being so cheap, there is no excuse for using the solution once it has lost its power.

When sterilizing bottles, jars, and so on, put about a quarter of a pint of solution into the first bottle (about a pint to a gallon jar), and shake the bottle (or jar) well so that all the inside is wetted. Then pour the solution into the next bottle, and so on until all have been treated. After you have finished, return the solution to the bulk for future use. Treat bottles and jars as they are required for use, and use them as soon as they have been treated. Before putting wine into them, drain them of solution and rinse them inside with a little cool, boiled water.

Sulphite solution is intended mainly for use with vessels and utensils that cannot be boiled—such as glass and plastic. But it is also useful for other things as well. Straining cloth, for example, can be sterilized with it. Afterwards they should be wrung out as dry as possible, shaken well, and then spread out to dry. Spoons and smaller implements, however, are best sterilized by dipping in boiling water.

When removing bungs from stored wine, or when removing a fermentation lock and bung, it is a wise precaution to wipe round the bung, and then the whole of the jar with a cloth well wetted with sulphite solution. This is because while the jars have been standing, dust, bacteria, yeast and mould spores will have been collecting on the surfaces. These can very easily contaminate the wine if precautions are not taken.

Using the Hydrometer

A great many more people would use the hydrometer if only they felt confident that they could, in fact, use it. So let me explain that it is no more difficult to use than a thermometer.

You use a thermometer to measure temperature, be it of air or liquids or your own when you are ill. As most of you already know, you use a hydrometer to measure sugar content – to find out how much sugar a must contains and how much sugar is being used up from day to day by the yeast in a fermenting must.

In the first instance, knowing how much sugar the must contains before the yeast is added allows us to calculate in advance how much alcohol that sugar will make and whether the wine will be sweet or dry when fermentation is complete. It also allows us to add the right amount of sugar required to make the type of wine we want. Without it, we would have to take chances all along the line and most likely finish up with a wine quite different from what we wanted.

In the second instance, we can not only determine in advance the amount of alcohol we shall make, but also determine later whether we have actually made it.

All this is of the utmost importance in these days when everybody is seeking to produce quality wines consistently and, as is now the case, when more and more people are developing a liking for dry wines.

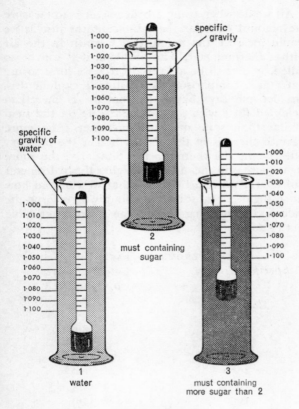

specific gravity

specific gravity of water

1·000
1·010
1·020
1·030
1·040
1·050
1·060
1·070
1·080
1·090
1·100

1·000
1·010
1·020
1·030
1·040
1·050
1·060
1·070
1·080
1·090
1·100

1·000
1·010
1·020
1·030
1·040
1·050
1·060
1·070
1·080
1·090
1·100

1
water

2
must containing
sugar

3
must containing
more sugar than 2

The Hydrometer

In these illustrations the scale which appears on the hydrometer in the normal way has been put beside the trial jar so that the scale can be enlarged for easy reading.

Bearing in mind that $2\frac{1}{4}$ oz sugar represents 5° on the hydrometer, we can easily work out how much sugar the two sample musts in this illustration contain.

All we do when using a hydrometer is to measure the amount of sugar the must contains just as we would measure the amount of warmth in the air with a thermometer. The problem, if it can be so called, is that to be able to do this we have to use water as a comparison. But before I explain this, just let me say that a hydrometer is merely a weighted float with a graduated scale on the stem similar to a scale on a thermometer. The more warmth there is in the air the higher the mercury will rise in the thermometer. Similarly, the more sugar there is in the must, the higher the hydrometer will float. And it is from this that we can find how much sugar the must contains simply by reading the scale and comparing it with the hydrometer table on this page.

HYDROMETER TABLE

Specific Gravity	Potential Alcohol by volume %
1020	2·4
1030	3·6
1040	5·0
1050	6·4
1060	7·7
1070	9·0
1080	10·5
1090	11·9
1100	13·4
1110	14·5
1120	16·0

From this table you will see how much sugar the must contains, how much alcohol this amount of sugar will make, and how much sugar to add to make the amount of alcohol you want. It is as simple as that. Examples appear later so that everything will become abundantly clear.

I have said that we must use water as a comparison. If we did not, we would not know where to begin. On one of the most widely used hydrometers the scale goes from 1·000 to 1·100. These figures indicate *specific gravity*—the density of the liquid as compared with the density of water. The reading of 1·000 therefore represents the gravity of water. So when the hydrometer floats in pure water, it floats at the 1·000 mark.

When you add sugar to water, you produce a syrup, which gets denser as you add more sugar. That is, the specific gravity rises. So when you put your hydrometer into the syrup, it will rise higher than if it were put into pure water. The amount it rises will, of course, depend on how much sugar you have added. Exactly the same applies to fruit juices. The hydrometer reading is an indication of the amount of sugar in the juice.

In the diagram on page 55 we see three hydrometers side by side. One is floating in pure water and shows a specific gravity of 1·000. The other two are floating in fruit juices with differing amounts of sugar present. If you now look at the hydrometer table on page 56, you will at once see how much alcohol the two amounts of sugar will produce.

Just to help you get used to reading the tables, the specific gravity of 1·030 will produce 3·6% of alcohol by volume, while the reading of 1·050 will give you 6·4% by volume. (The difference between alcohol by volume and per cent proof is explained on page 137.)

By far the best way to become familiar with using the hydrometer is to make up a must of fruit juice and water, as detailed in one of the recipes, and add to it an initial 2 lb of sugar. The fruit juice will contain some sugar itself, and this can be measured at the same time. But this will be very little when English garden or wild fruits are being used.

You should have at least one gallon of must. If you are intending to make one gallon of wine, you need only have $8\frac{1}{2}$ to 9 pints of must. The reason for having at least a gallon is this. When you take a hydrometer reading and read off the amount of sugar present from the hydrometer table, this amount of sugar is calculated on the basis of one gallon. For example, if you are making one, two or twenty gallons, the hydrometer reading and table will show you the amount of sugar in each gallon. If you have a three-gallon batch and the specific gravity is 1·070, the reading would be the same for each gallon if you made three separate gallon lots of it. The same applies to however many gallons the batch consists of.

But it does not apply to a measure totalling less than one gallon if you are subsequently going to make it up to a gallon. For example, if you have a must of three-quarters of a gallon with a reading of 1·070 when you make this into one gallon, you reduce the reading, simply because you have increased the dilution of the sugar and lowered the specific gravity. (Of course, the same thing occurs if you dilute any quantity of must after you have taken a reading.)

So start with a must of at least a gallon. As I have mentioned, the simplest way is to make up a must

using fruit juice and water and 2 lb of sugar. It does
not matter if it is just over the gallon. Three-parts
fill the trial jar with a sample of the must and stand
it on a level surface. Having done this, slowly slide
the hydrometer into the sample. If the sample overflows, do not worry. If the hydrometer does not float,
add more must until it does.

Now take the reading. Note the figure where the
sample cuts across the scale; this is the specific
gravity of your must. Now what could be simpler
than that? If you now look at the hydrometer table
on page 56, you will see at once that this figure will
produce such and such a percentage of alcohol by
volume. Now, in the usual way, especially where
bone-dry wines are required, less than the maximum
amount of alcohol the yeast will make is sufficient
because bone-dry wines should not be too strong.

But I am willing to bet that the amount of
alcohol the must will produce indicated by the reading, will not be enough and that you will want to
make the maximum. If this is so, then, obviously,
you will have to add some sugar to raise the specific
gravity to 1·110.

All you have to remember is that $2\frac{1}{4}$ oz of sugar
will raise the gravity by 5° on the hydrometer – $4\frac{1}{2}$
oz will raise it by 10°, and so on. Therefore for
each 5° that you want to raise the reading you must
add $2\frac{1}{4}$ oz of sugar. If you want to raise it by 15° then
the amount of sugar to add is three times $2\frac{1}{4}$ oz, or
$6\frac{3}{4}$ oz.

The best way to add sugar is to do so without
using water, which would otherwise have to be taken
into account and extra sugar added to allow for it.

To do this take a very small sample of the must in a china or polythene jug and add the sugar. Stand this in a saucepan of water over heat and warm gently, stirring until the sugar is dissolved. Then stir this syrup into the bulk and you have a must containing the amount of sugar you require to make the amount of alcohol you want. But on no account take the reading again because the small amount of sugar added will have increased the overall amount of wine by a tiny bit, and this will alter slightly the reading you should have obtained. But this will not matter because the end product will be what you aimed at provided that fermentation is satisfactory.

The foregoing applies to making dry wines where the specific gravity should not be more than 1·110 at the outset. Indeed, for dry wines, which are often better for being lower in alcohol than most others, a specific gravity of 1·100 at the start is usually plenty. But a lot depends on personal preference.

Now let us see what happens to a must prepared as described after fermentation has begun until it ceases. As most of you will know, fermentation may last for several months, or it may be over in a matter of weeks. In Fermentation Chart No. 1 (p. 20), I have tried to give a reasonably representative picture of the progress of fermentation. But do not expect your ferments to progress in an identical fashion. This is merely an illustration of what might happen under ordinary home conditions.

As soon as fermentation begins, there is some natural warming of the must because of yeast action. This can lead you to think that an appreciable drop in sugar content has taken place in the first day. What happens is this. The must expands slightly as it gets warmer, and this lowers its density and therefore a hydrometer reading if one is taken. So do not take a reading of the must until a week after fermentation has begun. By that time the temperature of the must will be reasonably normal. If you are using a fermentation cupboard, where the temperature of the must will be around 60° F, the warming effect will not be noticeable.

In the example of fermentation I have illustrated in Fermentation Chart No. 1 (p. 20), you will see that the hydrometer reading has dropped from 1·110 to 1·000. This is merely representative. The fact is that the reading when all fermentation has ceased might well be below 1·000. This is because all sugar has been fermented out and alcohol is now present. Alcohol is lighter than water, and therefore, it could very well be that a well-fermented dry wine would have specific gravity lower than that of water. In this case your hydrometer would sink to just below the 1·000 mark.

When you get a drop of 0·110 it means that you have made the amount of alcohol you wanted. But if you find that fermentation has stopped and that the reading is above 1·000, it means that you have not made the amount of alcohol you wanted, and you have not got the bone-dry wine you aimed at. You should therefore try to get fermentation going again in order to use up the little sugar that is left.

However, if you are satisfied with the wine as it is, there will be no need to do this. In any case, if there are only, say, 5° registering on the hydrometer at this stage, I doubt whether you will be able to get fermentation started again. You can, of course, leave the lock in place and keep the wine warm and hope

C

that fermentation recommences on its own – which it will often do – or regard the wine as a finished product ready for putting away to clear.

In Fermentation Chart No. 1 (p. 20), I have shown that fermentation ceased completely in twelve weeks. This is merely an example, so do not think there is something wrong if your ferments are of shorter or longer duration. From this chart you are able to see how the sugar is being used up and how, as this happens, the amount of alcohol increases. And I do urge readers to take weekly readings to see just how matters are progressing, for this can be quite fascinating and can add a useful measure of background knowledge for the future.

SPECIAL NOTES ON USING THE HYDROMETER

Having explained the use of the hydrometer in various aspects of wine-making, I want to bring home to those who simply must insist upon absolute accuracy, that certain points must be considered. The majority of wine-makers will be content to go ahead on the readings they obtain when finding the specific gravity of their musts and be quite content with the result of the fermentation and wine resulting from it. But it would be unfair if I were not to let others know that there are small factors which should be taken into account if they insist upon accuracy.

The illustration on page 63 shows an enlarged section of the hydrometer in a sample must. In this is illustrated what we call *surface tension*. Simply, what we mean by this is that sugar solutions – and even water to a lesser extent – tend to climb a little way up the stem of the hydrometer. The greater the sugar content, the higher is the surface tension.

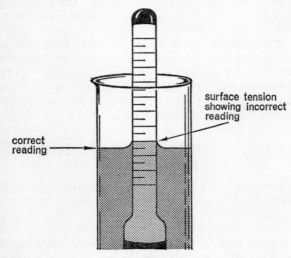

correct
reading

surface tension
showing incorrect
reading

Surface Tension

So when taking readings, take care to read the hydrometer strictly at eye level, and watch carefully for surface tension. Another factor is that, as most of you already know, a must is not made up merely of sugar and water. Neither are fruit juices. There are other constituents which have a small effect upon the hydrometer readings.

For example, the acids and pectin in fruits tend to increase the reading slightly. To allow for this, it is wise to regard the sugar content as being 3°

lower than the reading states. This would be ample
for musts containing the usual four or five pounds
of fruit to the gallon. But when, say, eight or more
pounds are used and when grapes are being fermented, it would be wise to allow as much as 5°
and deduct this from the reading.

Where dried fruits alone are being used, this al-
lowance is not necessary, but if equal quantities of
dried and fresh fruits are being used, half the figures
quoted would be enough, depending on whether
you are using ordinary English garden or wild fruits
or grapes with the dried fruits.

USING THE HYDROMETER WHEN MAKING SWEET WINES

Making sweet wines is more successful when the
hydrometer is used. I say this because it is always
best to start off with a specific gravity of 1·110. And
by using the hydrometer we are able to start with
the right amount of sugar in the must. How much
sugar the must contains before you add any depends
on the sugar content of the fruit and the amount of
fruit used. With English garden and wild fruits the
amount will be very little, but it is worth knowing
how much.

When making sweet wines we do exactly the same
as described for dry wines to start with. We start
fermentation in the normal way and watch its progress by taking readings with the hydrometer. These
need not be frequent; weekly or fortnightly will do.
Meanwhile, we must try to decide how much sugar
left unfermented will make a wine medium sweet
or sweet. This will depend a very great deal on

personal taste. A wine which is medium dry to medium sweet to one person may be sweet to another, and so on. Some people like a sweet wine with only 10° of sugar left registering as unfermented on the hydrometer. As we have seen, this 10° represents $4\frac{1}{4}$ oz of sugar. But others would want more than this.

So it is a matter of trial and error according to personal taste as to how much sugar to add in addition to the amount that will be used in making the alcohol we want. So we begin the ferment with a reading of 1·110, knowing that this amount of sugar will be fermented out in making the alcohol we want, and, as some sugar is used up, we add a little more. This extra will be left unfermented and will register on the hydrometer when all fermentation has ceased. In Fermentation Chart No. 2 on page 23, you will see exactly what I mean. You will see that with Ferment No. 1 we began with a reading of 1·110, and when the reading dropped to 1·060 we added $4\frac{1}{2}$ oz of sugar. This raised the reading from 1·060 to 1·070.

Now it is a fact that by adding sugar bit by bit we seem to be able to induce the yeast to make a little more alcohol than it otherwise might. But this is not something that you should count on, although it often happens. So you should always work on the assumption that you will not make more than 15% of alcohol by volume. If you do make more alcohol, and more sugar is used up in consequence, so much the better. But then you will have to add a little more sugar to give the wine the sweetness you want.

The effect of this is shown in Fermentation Chart

No. 2 as Ferment No. 2. In this we made two additions: one of $4\frac{1}{2}$ oz (10°) when the reading had fallen to 1·050, thereby raising it to 1·060; and another of $2\frac{1}{4}$ oz (5°) when the reading had dropped to 1·040, raising the reading to 1·045. In both cases we obtain a total drop of 0·110.

USING THE HYDROMETER WITH PULP FERMENTS

Pulp ferments as we call them are fruit musts fermented on the pulp, or where the fruits are crushed and the skins and pips fermented for a time.

To take an accurate reading (to obtain the correct specific gravity), you will have to crush the fruit well, and mix it with water, as in the many recipes and methods describing this type of ferment. Add the initial 2 lb of sugar with the remainder of the water, and then take a sample of the must. Strain out the solids through several thicknesses of muslin. You only need enough liquid to fill the trial jar. You can then make any adjustment required merely by consulting the other parts of this section.

The above applies to all garden and wild fruits. Musts made from grapes only are handled a little differently. This is because they contain a great deal of sugar – so much so, in fact, that it is always best to find the specific gravity before adding any sugar at all. It is a fact that some grapes, especially in a good season, will contain enough sugar to make an excellent dry wine without adding any sugar at all. But we cannot rely on this, so we must find out the specific gravity of the juice before we begin. And here a hydrometer which reads from 1·000 to 1·100 will suffice. Grapes are usually used alone and the juice left undiluted. Grapes bought from a green-grocer would make the cost of wine prohibitive – though some people seem able to afford it.

At this point I can let you into a little dodge that often works – I have done it late on a Saturday evening in certain London markets. Street traders packing up for the weekend will often sell off the remainder of their grapes at much less than the quoted price because they know that by the Monday – a day on which there is little demand for such fruit – the grapes will be past their best and by the Tuesday quite unsaleable. I have bought boxes containing more than fourteen pounds, marked up at three shillings a pound, for as little as twenty shillings. But you will have to bargain with them; otherwise they will diddle you with a smile and a conscience as clear as brilliant wine. I consider a gallon of top-class wine for twenty shillings well worthwhile.

It is impossible to say with any certainty how many pounds of grapes are required to make one gallon of wine. This is because the juice content will vary with each sort. This is dealt with elsewhere in this book. All we are concerned with in this section is finding the specific gravity of the juice of the grapes.

The first thing to do, therefore, is to crush them well by hand and wring them out by the handful in order to get all the sugar into the juice. The fact that the pulp is not strained from the juice does not matter. When the grapes are thoroughly crushed, take a small sample of the juice and strain it through several thicknesses of muslin. Put this into the hydrometer jar, and take the reading as for other juices.

You are then able to work out how much sugar you need to add to bring the specific gravity up to 1·110 (or 1·100 if this suits you), simply by looking up the details for other wines in this chapter. If you want to make sweet wines from grapes, you will tell at once by reading the appropriate section how adding sugar during fermentation affects the readings and how to calculate how much sugar is being used and the amount of alcohol you have made when all fermentation has ceased.

USING THE HYDROMETER WITH CONCENTRATED GRAPE JUICE

When using the hydrometer to make wines with concentrated grape juice, we work in a slightly different manner from those already described. And I think it is grape juices and their high specific gravity that have made it difficult for many readers to grasp the simple use of the hydrometer. I say this because I have had so many queries from people who could not understand the action of the hydrometer when diluting a heavy concentrate with water.

Now, most concentrated grape juices are reputed to have a specific gravity anywhere between 1·380 and 1·400. And if we could believe the figure stated by the producer, all would be well – but we cannot do this.

Retailers usually quote the specific gravity of their grape juices on information provided by their wholesalers, so they are not necessarily to blame for inaccuracies. But this means that before we can hope to make wines successfully with them we must find out how much sugar the concentrate contains before we begin. This will vary with the source of supply, the country of origin and the variety of the grapes. Some concentrates come in polythene containers in the form of heavy black syrup – or white syrup in the case of white grape concentrate for white wines – while others are solid and packed in tins.

As a general rule, one quart of concentrate will make one gallon of top-class wine. When you have concentrate on hand, you can start work to find out how much sugar it contains. The best plan to begin with is to make one quart of concentrate into half a gallon. This will reduce the specific gravity.

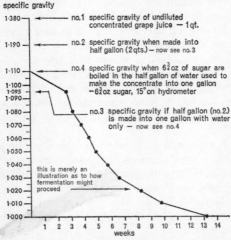

Chart Illustrating Dilution of Concentrated Grape Juice

Here, alas, is where so many beginner-users of the hydrometer become so puzzled. They expect a specific gravity of 1·380 to be reduced to half that figure, 0·690, when the concentrate is diluted with its own quantity of water. They overlook the fact that water itself has a specific gravity of 1·000 and that the sugar content only affects the reading above the 1·000, in this case, 0·380.

After giving talks to various wine-making circles, during which many people have told me that they use the hydrometer for every wine they make, other members have taken me aside about the hydrometer because they do not like to appear ignorant of the subject to other members. While this attitude is pathetically short-sighted, it is understandable, and this is one reason why this book is so necessary. Everybody wants to learn, yet nobody wants to appear ignorant in front of anybody else.

As I have said, the best plan is to make one quart of concentrate into half a gallon by mixing it well with a quart of boiled water that has the chill off. On no account use hot water. Having done this, take the reading with a hydrometer which reads from 1·100 to 1·200. If your concentrate had a specific gravity of 1·380 you should now have a reading of 1·190.

But it does not matter what specific gravity the concentrate was claimed to have, because you can very easily find out what it was by doubling the reading you now have – but, remember, only the figure above the 1·000. Here it is wise to call a halt for a moment and look at the hydrometer table for grape concentrate on page 69. From this you will see at once that if you make your half gallon into one gallon by adding half a gallon of water, you will reduce your reading by half again.

You now know in advance what the specific gravity will be when the concentrate has been fully diluted to one gallon. If you look at the hydrometer table on page 56, you will see how much alcohol you will make and be able to calculate how much sugar to add to give you the reading you want to start with.

In my example in the hydrometer table for grape concentrates, I have given the figure 1·095 as the reading of the concentrate when made into one gallon. Your concentrate may give a different reading from this by a degree or two either way. But this will not matter because you can easily work out the little difference that this will make.

Now as I have said, it is always best to start with a specific gravity of 1·110 (or 1·100 if making dry wines). So all you have to do when you know in advance what the specific gravity of the diluted concentrate will be is to work out how much sugar you will have to add to make the reading up to 1·110 (or 1·100). The whole point of finding out what the reading will be in advance of diluting to the full is so that you can boil this extra sugar in the water you use to dilute the concentrate.

By working in this way, you do not have to add sugared water to the fully diluted concentrate. If you did, you would dilute the grape juice a little more than you need. In other words, if you dilute to the full extent and then have to add, say, half a pound of sugar, you will have to dissolve this in an extra half pint or pint of water. This would affect the overall quality of the wine and throw out of line your earlier calculations.

In the example we are considering here, we have found out in advance the specific gravity will be 1·095 when fully diluted. We must now increase the reading to 1·110 (or 1·100, if this suits you better). So, in that half gallon of water that is to be used to make the concentrate into one gallon, you will have to boil either 4½ oz sugar to raise it by 10°, or 6¾ oz to raise it by 15° as in my example. Your own figures with the particular concentrate you are using will vary slightly from mine, but it is simplicity itself to work out how much sugar you need. All you have to remember is that 2¼ oz of sugar will raise the specific gravity 5° on the hydrometer.

After you have got your gallon of grape juice to the right sweetness, you proceed as for other wines. If you look at the fermentation tables for dry and sweet wines on pages 20 and 23, you will see at once how to handle your grape-juice wine after starting the fermentation, according to whether you want dry or sweet wine.

USING THE HYDROMETER FOR BEER AND SPARKLING WINES

Using the hydrometer in beer-making is very similar to using it in wine-making. Those of you making ordinary draught beers need not use it at all if you would rather not. But if you want to be sure of the amount of alcohol you aimed at, you will need a hydrometer.

You must start with a specific gravity that will

produce the alcohol you want and then, at the end, take a reading to find whether you have in fact made the amount required. Now, in the normal way, when making beers we begin with a specific gravity of between 1·050 and 1·070. If you look at the hydrometer table on page 56, you will see that these readings will make 6·4% and 9·0% of alcohol by volume, respectively. There is no need to start with a specific gravity of above 1·070, because 9·0% alcohol is quite strong enough for beers. Indeed, many people prefer beers lower in alcohol than this, especially during the warmer weather when lighter beers are more popular.

Of course, we shall always have among us those few who simply must have their beers stronger than average, and that is their affair. But, on the whole, over-strong beers serve no purpose other than to produce colossal hangovers and bad tempers.

We have only to look at Fermentation Chart No. 1 to see how beers ferment from the original specific gravity to 1·000 in a week or so. In the example we began with a specific gravity of 1·050. If we had started with a specific gravity of 1·060 or 1·070, it would take only a day or two longer for fermentation to reduce the reading to 1·000. These examples, you must understand, are *examples* only. You will find that your own brews will react differently. This is because no two brews react in an identical fashion, as I explained under 'Fermentation,' p. 17.

In beer-making, it is wise to begin with a reliable recipe that will produce a beer of flavour. Then take a reading. If this is below the reading that will make the amount of alcohol you want, add sugar accordingly. Remember that, as for wines, 2¼ oz of sugar

will raise the specific gravity by 5° on the hydrometer, and so on.

It is very simple to get the right specific gravity
for beers and to ferment them to completion, that is,
to 1·000, and to leave them as draught beers. But if
you want gaseous beers, that is, bottled beers, you
must work in a slightly different manner. But, and
this is important, before you make gaseous beers,
for your own sake, get a little experience in making
ordinary draught beer first. In this way you can become familiar with using the hydrometer.

When you are satisfied that you know what you
are doing, you can make bottled beers with confidence. Inexperienced beer-makers could run up
against all sorts of troubles including exploding
bottles, if they are not careful. This is not to say that
making bottled or gaseous beer is dangerous because
it is not, provided that you know and understand
the hydrometer and why it is used in making this
type of beer.

There are two methods of working when making
gaseous beers. In the first method, allow the beer to
ferment out to 1·000 and then add $2\frac{1}{4}$ oz of sugar to
each gallon, not forgetting to add the appropriate
amount for parts of a gallon. Put the beer into
screw-top bottles and screw the stoppers home.
Leave the beer in a warm place for three or four
days and then move it to a cool place. During the
time in the warm, fermentation will go on inside the
bottles and so charge the beer with all-important
gas. But the amount of sugar given is not high
enough to give rise to sufficient gas to burst the
bottles.

Indeed, a little more sugar may be used by experienced beer-makers to obtain more gas. But, owing to the effects of warmth on bottled beers, it is as well not to exceed $2\frac{1}{4}$ oz a gallon until you are very experienced, especially if you do not have a really cool place to store them. The warmth causes the beer in the bottles to expand and the pressure inside to increase. The result is that when you open the bottles, the beer shoots out and you lose most of it over the ceiling. So do not exceed $2\frac{1}{4}$ oz of added sugar per gallon, and do make sure before adding it that your beer has in fact fermented out to 1·000. If by some chance it stopped fermenting at, say 1·002, then you need to add a little less than $2\frac{1}{4}$ oz.

In the other method of making gaseous beers, take hydrometer readings regularly, especially during the last few days of fermentation, and siphon the beer into bottles when the reading has dropped to 1·005. Then screw down the stopper. If you do it this way you will be leaving $2\frac{1}{4}$ oz of sugar to ferment in the bottle.

When making gaseous beers it is of the utmost importance that as little yeast as possible is present in the bottles to start with. So the best plan is to use good beer-making yeasts. These settle well and quickly so that by the time fermentation has used up enough sugar to reduce the reading to 1·005—the time when the beer is put into bottles—there is very little yeast left in suspension. But there is still enough to carry on the fermentation necessary to charge the beer with gas. Siphoning the almost clear beer into bottles is the best plan as this ensures that the last bottle to be filled has more of the deposit from the bottom of the fermentation vessel accidentally poured into it.

The overriding importance of getting as near as possible clear beer into bottles is that, as fermentation uses up those last ounces of sugar, a little yeast is produced. This will stick to the bottom of the bottle so that all but the last few drops may be poured free from cloudiness. But this will be true only if a good beer yeast has been used.

You may ask how the trade get their bottled beers brilliantly clear and free of any suggestion of deposit. The simple answer is that they have the plant with which to do it. They ferment their beers to completion and bottle them free from all yeast. Then they charge the bottles with gas under pressure. I call that cheating. Those lovely bubbles that rise so invitingly in commercial beer are as false as a pair of dentures. Perhaps one day we shall have small plants available to wine- and beer-making clubs that will enable members to have a 'bottling night' when they will queue up to get their beers 'gassed'. But until such times arrive, we shall have to put up with matters as they are.

See an improved means of taking gravities with the Drake Trial Tube on page 165.

Enzyme Action in Beer-Making

When making beers we are more concerned with enzyme action than when making wines. This is because once we have prepared the must for wines we are no longer concerned with enzyme action other than that taking place during fermentation. This, as we have seen, is automatic in so far as it can be and we have nothing to do with it except to assist it. We do this by producing a must suitable for the full and complete enzyme action of the yeast and by giving the yeast the warmth it needs to secrete its enzymes satisfactorily.

However, when making beers we are concerned with enzyme action from the very beginning, not just from the beginning of preparing the wort, but from the moment when the barley is put through the first stages of malting. Agreed, we have nothing to do with this as we buy either malted barley (malt still within the grain, generally known simply as malt) or malt extract – as a syrup, dried in flakes, or as a powder.

Many beer-makers buy malt (malt still within the grain) and toast it under a grill to obtain special flavours. The beginner is unlikely to do this. Nevertheless, his beer-making becomes far more interesting if he knows something of the processes that produce the main ingredient of the beers he makes.

Malt extract in all its forms is the maltose extracted from the grain. It is the form of malt most

commonly used by home brewers because it relieves
them of one of the most difficult operations – that
of mashing. This is the process by which the malt is
extracted from the grain. A good deal of skill is required if this is to be done successfully. By using
malt already extracted, the home brewer begins half
way through the process of beer-making. This is why
beer-making has become so popular. It is so easy that
it is like using instant coffee instead of roasting and
grinding the beans and then making the coffee in a
percolator.

The first step in producing malt is to grow the
barley. This is done on a tremendous scale in this
country, and some of the best barley in the world is
produced here when the season has been good. The
seed of barley is rock-hard, but when it has been
malted it is so soft that you can crack it with gentle
pressure from your teeth. When you have done this,
you can clearly taste the malt.

When the barley has been harvested it is taken to
the malting houses – hundreds of tons at a time.
There it is spread on the malting floor where arti-
ficial growing conditions are produced. Like any
other seed, barley contains the germ of new life and
a supply of food for the plant that will grow from it.
This food is in the form of insoluble starches and
proteins which are not available to the new life
until new growth begins. Immediately this happens,
digestive fermentation (enzyme action) takes place
within the seed. This breaks down the proteins and
starches into materials that the plant can use for
growth.

The man who starts, controls and halts the malting process at the right time is called a maltster. First

he piles the barley into heaps and moistens it so that, like any other seed, it germinates and growth begins. He watches carefully for the growing point of the new plant to appear. While he waits, enzyme action in the form of digestive ferments are taking place and producing malt within the seed. The maltster gives the barley warmth and water until the growing point is about three parts along the seed. Then he slows down the growing process by withholding water from the seed and finally prevents all further growth by drying it.

Having judged the process of growth correctly and having halted it at the right time, the maltster has produced seed containing the maximum amount of malt. This is what we call malt, malted barley, or malt still within the grain. Malt extract, in whichever form it is obtained, is malt extracted from the seed. The amount of malt extracted from one seed can barely be seen. When you consider that thousands of tons of malt extract are used in this country alone each year, you wonder just how much barley must be grown to produce this.

All malt is more or less the same until it is treated to give more flavour and colour. Crystal malts are usually cooked in gas ovens. Some are roasted over wood fires. The lighter ales are produced from malts cooked very lightly in order to retain a light colour and flavour. Some home brewers buy malt still within the grain and roast it under a grill to obtain special results. In doing this, they are merely carrying on where the professional man left off.

During the process of beer-making more enzyme action takes place. The ground malt is first fed into mash tuns, where it is treated with prepared water –

otherwise known as brewery liquor. No-one ever uses the term 'water' in a brewery; it is always known as liquor. As soon as the malt is treated with brewery liquor, the enzyme action halted by the maltster when he dried the malt recommences. Digestive ferments take place once more to convert starches to sugar. Dextrins and maltodextrins are produced as well as rather less fermentable particles which all play their part in forming the character of the beer. Each enzyme comes into action at a certain temperature.

The first enzyme completes its task and, as the temperature rises, the second enzyme takes over, and so on. The brewer assists the process by raising the temperature at the right time. Too high a temperature at the wrong time could destroy the very sensitive enzymes. Returning the wort to the correct temperature after overheating would be useless as the enzymes would already have been destroyed. This is rather like cooking. If you overcook a joint through carelessness, you cannot restore the joint to what you wanted it to be by allowing it to cool because of the finality of the overcooking.

The brewer, therefore, carefully controls the temperature so that each enzyme does its work of conversion to the correct degree before the next enzyme is allowed to take over at a higher temperature. When the brewer is satisfied that all enzyme action has taken place satisfactorily, he boils the wort. This boiling 'fixes' the character of the beer. In other words, it stops all further enzyme action. The brewer boils the wort when he knows he has produced precisely the kind he needs for the sort of beer he is making, whether it be light ale, brown ale, pale ale, bitter or what have you.

The wort is then cooled by refrigeration equipment rather than naturally because of the danger of attacks from spoilage yeasts and bacteria. Boiling in the first instance destroyed any that might have been present. When the wort has cooled to a suitable temperature – usually about 60° F – yeast is 'pitched' in. Within hours the great transformation from flat, murky wort to brilliant foaming beer has begun. Thereafter, the action of yeast and its enzymes is very similar to that in wine-making.

Beer-making on these lines, if only in quantities of say five to ten gallons, is far beyond the scope of most home brewers, although a great many do brew on this scale. Luckily for them, they have facilities such as a scullery or semi-basement where this sort of thing can be carried on without inconvenience and where they have all the space they need. Such accommodation is becoming scarce and within a few years it will become rare because this type of house is gradually making way for more modern accommodation.

It is in the modern house that home brewing is carried on with the use of malt extract. This is almost as simple as using concentrated grape juice for making wines. First of all boil the maltose (malt extracted from the grain) with water. Boil your hops separately and combine the two to make the wort. Add the yeast, together with some citric acid and perhaps other additives such as yeast nutrient, and allow fermentation with its enzyme action to take place. During the process of fermentation you can decide whether you want draught or gaseous beer and work accordingly.

Enzyme action throughout fermentation is very similar to that during wine-making.

Correcting Faults and Blending

CORRECTING FAULTS

Correcting or adjusting faults in finished wines is all part of the know-how of wine-making, and herein lies many of the tricks of the trade together with many of the skills that go to make a clever wine-maker.

When making wines we set out to produce a certain type of product. Sometimes we succeed so easily that we are almost embarrassed by our good fortune. At other times, obtaining what we really want calls for some skill. Whatever our aim, we can obtain it, or get as near to it as is humanly possible without much trouble provided that we have a rough idea of what we want and how to set about getting it.

In the first place we use a recipe and method that will produce what we are after. But it sometimes happens that the end product is not quite what we wanted. There may be too much acid present, or the wine may be either too sweet or too dry. These are not really faults as such because whatever sort of wine you get, some will acclaim it the finest they have tasted while others will shudder at it. It is all a matter of taste, and surely the skill in making wines comes in making the type of variety you really like. This is easy enough when you have gained experience in making a wide variety of wines, even if it means treating the finished product in some way.

Make no mistake about this, your favourite commercial product whether it be wine or whisky could not be produced without after-treatment of some sort, usually blending. In the case of the higher-alcohol wines, such as ports and sherries, fortifying is also carried out because, like us, commercial producers cannot produce more alcohol than the yeast will make. If it were not for this, commercial products would not be stronger than those made by home wine-makers.

Over-acid Wines

An over-acid wine will naturally show itself by making you wince. The simplest means of reducing the acid in an over-acid wine is to blend it with a similar wine which lacks acid. Lack of acid is usually noticed as lack of bite, that is, having swallowed the wine, it is gone. There is nothing left on the palate to tell you that you have, in fact, tasted wine rather than something else with a fruity flavour. Obviously the blending improves both the wines – the over-acid and the under-acid.

But how do you reduce acidity if you have no wine lacking in acid? The simplest means of correcting this is to use pure medicinal chalk (precipitated chalk) from a chemist. This aspect is covered later under the heading 'Balance of Acid.' Under that we discuss removing acid from a must. In finished wines the operation is slightly different. First, it should be decided how much over-acid the wine is, and whether the fault is, in fact, over-acidity rather than harshness caused by an excess of tannin. It should be made clear, though, that young wines sometimes have a slightly acid and sometimes harsh taste as well. Therefore, young wines should never be treated, but should be kept until they are a year old. By that time many of the suspected faults will have ironed themselves out. If after a year a wine is still over-acid, then treatment with chalk is justified.

Put the wine into an open vessel such as a fermentation vessel, and treat a sample pint as described under 'Balance of Acid'. After treating the bulk with this doctored pint, allow the chalk to settle out until the wine is brilliant again before tasting.

If further treatment is necessary you can do this without removing the wine from the chalk deposit. After removing the required amount of acid, allow the wine to clarify to brilliance – which will take less than an hour – and then siphon it into bottles or a jar for further storage. If by accident, you remove too much acid, add a little citric or tartaric acid to make it up.

Rough Wines

Rough or harsh wines usually have a rather stronger all-round flavour than is wanted, with a noticeable harshness to the palate.

Certain fruit wines made from rather more fruit than usual will produce this type of fault. Elderberry is a notable offender in this respect. So it is wise to stick to a well-tried recipe and not exceed four pounds per gallon. This amount will not produce an excess of acid provided that all the fruits are ripe. Nor will this amount produce an excess of tannin provided that the pulp is not fermented for too long.

You will often find harshness in a new wine, but delay treatment for a year or so to enable self-rectification to take place if it will. Treating for roughness too soon, may result in a considerable lack of desirable characteristics when a treated wine has ironed out its own faults. The overall effects can be that twice the amount of roughness has been removed when half of it should have remained to give the wine necessary character.

When roughness persists after a year of storage, whisk half of the white of an egg into a froth with a little of the wine and stir it into the bulk. Allow to settle out and then taste the wine. If similar further treatment is necessary, do it before taking the wine off this first deposit. Be careful not to take out too much, although you remedy this by adding a pinch of grape tannin. Allow the treated wine to clarify to brilliance and then bottle it or put it into jars for further storage. The half of an egg white recommended is for the experimental treatment of one gallon. When treating larger amounts, increase the amount of egg-white accordingly.

When egg-white is added to the wine, it forms an insoluble cloud which surrounds tannin and other constituents causing the harshness and takes them to the bottom of the jar.

This treatment is necessary only with red wines, and then only rarely, but it is as well to know what to do.

BLENDING

As I think I have written elsewhere (I have written so much about this subject that half has been forgotten), I firmly believed in my early days that if

I made wine from elderberries or blackberries then it must be from these alone, without any addition of any sort.

I felt that if I could not make a good wine from these fruits alone, I had no business making wines at all. Besides, I believed that wine must be labelled according to the fruit used. However, my early prejudice against blending has been completely knocked for six by modern arguments and practice. Blending either the ingredients or the finished wines is now common, and it is very often the only means of achieving particular results.

This is not to say that top-class wines are not to be obtained from a single ingredient – they certainly are. For example, English wild and garden fruits and concentrated grape juice make top-class wines that satisfy the most educated palates without other ingredients being used. However, many ingredients do not make good wines by themselves. Take roots and flowers, for example. They must be blended with other ingredients, such as citrus fruits and dried fruits. Today, all good recipes include either or both of these with the basic ingredients. The end product is what counts. Bananas, too, must be blended with other ingredients.. To obtain special results, too, blending the finished wines is often the only answer. And it is very often the only means of correcting faults.

Very many wine-makers make large amounts of individual wines for the sole purpose of blending them. They make, for example, a large batch of dry wine, which is always the easiest to make. They keep, say, one gallon of this as dry. Then they blend the second gallon of the batch with a sweet wine made with different fruit to give them a medium-sweet wine of a varied type, and blend, say, a third gallon with some other wine. In this way, they know from experience that they will obtain the special results they are after which could not be produced in any other way – not even by blending the various fruits before making the wines.

Blending needs common sense and a sense of purpose. It is no use at all adding one wine to another just to see what happens. Due consideration should be given not only to what you want but also to whether the wines you are considering blending will give the results you are aiming at. Can I help you in this respect? I cannot, simply because I do not know what you are likely to want to achieve by blending.

All I can do is to tell you which wines will blend well to prevent you spoiling several good wines. On no account blend for the sake of blending as this sort of thing can lead to disappointment.

The simplest and the best way of blending is by using several glasses – for instance, take three rows of three glasses (a dilution of 1 in 3 will probably be quite enough for most blending purposes). In the first glass of each row put one teaspoonful of the first wine. In the second glass of each row put two teaspoonfuls of the first wine, and in the third, three. Then add one teaspoonful of the second wine to each glass in the first row (this will give you blends of 1:1, 2:1 and 3:1). Add two teaspoonfuls of the second wine to each glass in the second row (this gives you 1:2, 2:2, 3:2). And add three teaspoonfuls of the second wine to each glass in the third row (this gives you 1:3, 2:3, 3:3). You can

of course omit 2 : 2 and 3 : 3, which are the same as
1 : 1, but the other dilutions will give you seven
blends from which to choose. Sample each blend,
taking a small piece of cheese between samples to
clear the palate, and if you have chosen your two
wines carefully in the first place, one of the blends
will give you the result you are after.

When you have found it, you will know from
the number of teaspoonfuls of each wine used how
many bottles of each you need to make up half a
gallon or a gallon. When you have done this, put
the blended wine away for six months for the blends
to 'marry'. This is far more important than most
people imagine. Marrying or interweaving of the
various constituents, bouquets, esters, and so on,
takes time. When this is complete, the blended wine
should be of top quality.

The following groups of wines blend well with
each other:

GROUP 1	Black plum
	Elderberry
	Blackberry
	Damson
	Blackcurrant
	Bilberry (herts or blueberry)
	Mulberry
	Black grape – fruit or concentrate

Usually, only two wines are needed, but three and
sometimes even four may be used.

Raspberry
White grape (fruit or concentrate)
Mulberry
Loganberry
Damson
GROUP 2   Redcurrant
Whitecurrent
Dried fruit wines – except elderberry
    and bilberry
Sloe – fresh or dried

Rhubarb
Dried fruit wines – except elderberry,
GROUP 3   sloe and bilberry
Root wines – except beetroot

Oversweet white fruit wines blend well with a little rhubarb. Certain wines that may be lacking in acid – but not red wines – also blend well with rhubarb.

Peach
Apricot
GROUP 4   White grape – fresh fruit or concentrate

Flower wines rarely blend well either with themselves or with fruit wines. But a dash of rhubarb wine has been known to improve them. Some winemakers, however, maintain that they obtain very excellent blends of flower wines. But there will always be someone to contradict me.

In any event, blending should not be resorted to for its own sake. If you have really good wines that can stand on their own feet and knock people off theirs, why try to improve them? Seriously, though, blending for the sake of it can not only irrevocably spoil really good wines but also disappoint the blender.

The same applies to blending ingredients. Once you have found a good recipe that makes the wine you like, it is wise to leave the recipe as it is. But if you really feel that the wine would have been just that much better if there had been a little more of 'this' or perhaps a little less of 'that', then there is absolutely no reason at all for not altering the blend of ingredients to suit your own taste. Or you can even add an ingredient not included in the recipe.

I have evolved hundreds of recipes by doing just this sort of thing, taking into account that one ingredient will add fruitiness, another body and some bouquet, another acid, and yet another tannin, all in suitable proportions. Judging by the popularity of my recipes – which have produced wines that have and still do win prizes all over the country, my choice of ingredients has been reasonably good.

This is not to say that I am infallible – I have turned out some pretty disappointing wines at times. But this is, of course, how I obtained my knowledge. Any wine-maker wishing to evolve his own recipes must take into account the constituents necessary in an initial must and in a finished wine. If he does and bears in mind the types of ingredients that will put these constituents into a must, he will, with practice, evolve some excellent recipes.

Racking, 'Off' Flavours, and Clarifying Problems

RACKING AND 'OFF' FLAVOURS

Racking is the term used to describe decanting, or removing wines from deposit that gradually build up during fermentation. These deposits are made up of minute particles of fruit (or vegetable where roots are employed) and dead yeast cells.

During the early stages of fermentation a great deal of new yeast is made and a great deal of unwanted fruit pulp with this yeast settles to the bottom of the vessel. A little of both, however, are kept in suspension by the agitation caused by the upsurge of carbon dioxide bubbles. The heavier solids forming the lees at this stage are too heavy to be kept in suspension.

Lying at the bottom, the fruit particles and yeast cells are subject to autolysis after a time. This is caused by what we might call 'further enzyme action'. (We have seen under the heading 'Fermentation', that enzymes play an important part in this process.)

It is at this stage, when much of the yeast is dead and when there is a deposit of particles of vegetable matter, that further enzyme action causes decomposition of both. And, as you know, anything decomposing is likely to give off smells. In the case of wines this decomposing matter is undoubtedly the cause of the development of what we call 'off' flavours. Difficult as there are to describe, you can detect them at once when you taste the wine. To avoid this unpleasant occurrence, periodic racking is desirable. But unnecessary disturbance should be avoided—by this, I mean racking every few weeks or so. This is quite unnecessary. Wine-makers with a good deal of experience will know almost instinctively when to rack and when to leave alone.

In the normal way, a method of making wines will include racking in the early stages of production in its scope of operations. For example, ten or fourteen days after yeast is added to the must and fermentation begun, the must is put into jars and the deposit left in the fermenting vessels. This is the first racking. Thereafter, the wine is allowed to carry on fermenting under fermentation locks, and new deposits build up.

The need to remove this second deposit is not so urgent simply because, when the first racking took place, almost all vegetable matter was removed and a much smaller yeast colony was left to carry on the ferment. And this is why fermentation is far slower than during the early stages.

In the normal way, further racking should not be carried out for eight to ten weeks, unless a heavier-than-average deposit is building up. Normally, the yeast is not coloured by the fruit being used. So if you find that you have a deposit building up quickly and that this is coloured, it means that you have a good deal of fruit particles in the deposit. So do not delay removal of these longer than is necessary.

D

Racking in this fashion assists clarification. But racking should not be mistakenly used as a means of clarifying. Bear in mind that wines will not clear while there is still fermentation going on. Admittedly, I have had wines as brilliantly clear as they will ever become with occasional gas bubbles rising lazily to the surface. But there will always be exceptions to the rule, as experienced wine-makers will know.

As fermentation slows down over a period of time, the deposit likely to build up will be slight indeed. The initial racking will rid the must of the more troublesome deposits, and the second racking will take care of any remaining deposits that may cause trouble. Thereafter the build-up should be very slight, and this need not be cause for alarm.

Whether or not to rack to remove this fine deposit when the wine is put away to finish clearing at the cessation of fermentation depends to a great extent on the clarity of the wine. If the wine is near-brilliant, there should be no need to rack at this stage because it will be only a matter of weeks (or even days) before the last of the minute solids in suspension have finally settled out. Then, and only then, should the wine be racked into storage jars, free from all deposit. This operation should be done by siphoning (see p. 105).

If, however, there is a quarter inch or more of deposit and the wine is still cloudy when fermentation has ceased, it would be wise to rack before putting the wine away to clear. This is advisable in case the wine takes longer than usual to become brilliant, in which event the wine would be left on the deposit longer than is desirable.

When brilliant wine is put away for storing, it is generally thought that no more deposits will form. Unfortunately, this is not the case. Very often – indeed, more often than not – wines will throw deposits even though they were brilliant to the eye when put away. When the wine is in stone jars or barrels it is impossible to tell whether further deposits have occurred because we cannot see through these as we can see through glass.

It is therefore a good plan when storing wines in stone jars or barrels to fill half a bottle with the wine to be stored and cork and seal it as if it were a finished product. Label it so that you know which bulk lot it belongs to and then, after three or four months, examine the bottom of the bottle carefully. If there are deposits there, however slight, there will be slightly heavier deposits in the bulk lot. This will be evidence of the need to rack.

Sometimes, with very dark glass bottles it is difficult to detect whether there is a deposit or not. If this problem arises, hold the wine up to bright light and twist the bottle sharply. If a deposit is present, it will rise up into the wine like a cloud of smoke.

Sweet wines, it must be understood, are often slower to clear than others – especially the very sweet ones. This is because the sugar present is in more or less the form of syrup and this, naturally, tends to slow down the settling out of the almost weightless solids.

You will appreciate that after each racking there is certain to be a little less wine. It is therefore advisable to put the wine into smaller containers each time, even if this means using half-gallon jars rather than larger vessels. This will mean that the advantages of bulk storing are lost. But the alternative is to store the wine with a large air-space above it. Since this air-space can lead to bacterial infection, I know which alternative I prefer. Hence my recommendations in my other works and magazine articles (where I gave recipes for making one-gallon lots) to put half in a half-gallon jar and bottle the remainder. This almost stock ending to my magazine recipes is a bit of a stock joke among the knowledgable wine-makers. But they do agree that it is better than storing with a large air-space above the wine.

Many wine-makers anxious to store in bulk for as long as possible prefer to make more than one gallon, say about a gallon and a quarter or perhaps a little more, or, say, an extra quart to each gallon actually required when all the processes have finished. This little extra is kept fermenting separate from the bulk and is used to top it up after each racking. In this way, whether it be one or five gallons that they want to set aside for storage, they may do so without having to leave an air-space overhead. This sort of thing is a trick-of-the-trade that people think up for themselves.

CLARIFYING

In the normal way, wines clarify to brilliance without assistance of any sort, except periodic racking. This is because the method used, rather than the recipes or the type of ingredients, was the sort that does not allow for pectin or starch to appear in the must. These substances are the two most troublesome and most common causes of nonclarification.

As we have just seen, the larger particles of fruit pulp and the heavier yeast particles settle out in the early stages to form the initial heavy deposit. Even the lighter solids will settle out when the upsurge of carbon dioxide gas produced during fermentation ceases. Later, the almost weightless solids settle out. They are too light to settle out by themselves, but eventually they join up to form heavier particles and fall to the bottom of the jar. Thus, wines made by methods that do not allow the presence of pectin or starch in the must will not present a clarifying problem.

When starch or pectin are present, they form a barrier which prevents the almost weightless solids from joining up to become heavier. In this way they prevent the solids from settling out. The problem is increased by the fact that the clarifiers used to clear wines not affected by starch or pectin will have no effect on these two substances except, in certain cases, to worsen matters.

The effect of most clarifying agents is to form an insoluble cloud which surrounds the minute solids, bringing them together so that they become heavy enough to settle out. Isinglass, and gelatine (two tricky substances) and the white of an egg are commonly used for this purpose, but they are quite useless against pectin or starch.

The presence of pectin in a wine is almost certainly due to a faulty method of production. Pectin is found in all fruits in varying quantities. Heating the fruit releases acid which, in turn, releases the pectin. This is why the sulphiting process for fruit is so popular – it does not involve such problems. Wines produced by this method have the flavour of the raw fruit, which is most popular. But those who like wines with a stewed-fruit flavour often boil the fruits or juices. If not for this reason, they boil them to destroy the wild yeast and bacteria present. Thus they sterilize their fruit but give themselves the problem of pectin hazes.

Certain fruits produce so much pectin that wines made by the heating process have a cloudiness as dense as that found in fruit cordials. This is because the more pectin there is present, the heavier are the solids held in suspension by it. The same applies to starch. Those who must boil their fruit must use either a pectin-destroying enzyme at the start or later to destroy the pectin and allow the almost weightless solids to join up and settle out. The use of starch- and pectin-destroying enzymes will be discussed later.

Those who like wines with a stewed-fruit flavour have the choice of using a pectin-destroying enzyme or a method that prevents the release of the pectin into the must. And the only means of doing this is to crush the fruit and put it through a jelly bag to remove, prior to boiling, all fruit particles which contain pectin.

When this method is being used, time should be allowed after the fruit has been gathered for enzymes in the fruit to start their work. This is important if the maximum amount of juice is to be obtained. For example, you will find that a soft fruit, such as a gooseberry or a plum, left on a plate in a warm place for a day or so will begin to exude juice of its own accord. This is evidence that enzyme action has broken down the juice-bearing tissues.

This action can be speeded up in a prepared fruit

mixture by using a commercially produced enzyme. The object of this is to speed up chemical changes in the fruit that would otherwise take much longer. Fruits or fruit pulps treated in this fashion produce much more free-running juice. This has a fresher flavour which is imparted to the wine. Also, because it is free-running, it passes through the jelly bag quickly. Juice prepared in this way may be boiled without fear of pectin hazes clouding the wine.

But in the normal way, unless you insist upon wines with the flavour of cooked or partially cooked fruit, it is best to use a method that does not call for heating the fruit or juices.

Roots, of course, are a different matter. Potatoes, parsnips and carrots must be boiled in order to destroy soil bacteria. Therefore, pectin as well as starch is boiled into the must. Usually there is so little pectin that this presents no clarifying problem. Starch, however, is a different matter. This will cause the same kind of trouble as pectin. But if a very little sugar is added to the must prior to adding the yeast, an enzyme in the yeast will convert the starch to sugar so that the yeast is able to ferment it. In this way the starch is removed. In these circumstances, the starch boiled into the must cannot produce a clarifying problem.

The amount of sugar to add would depend on the amount of wine being made, but two or three ounces per gallon would suffice to encourage the yeast to turn to starch for sustenance.

The making of root wines is now very much on the decline because there are so many ingredients available which require much less preparation. There are, for example, the usual English garden and wild fruits; tinned pulps and juices; dried fruits of many kinds, in addition to those normally found in the shops – raisins, sultanas, and currants; and special extracts and flavourings. All this adds up to modern wine-making from tinned, packeted and bottled ingredients. Readers of my 'Home Wine-making all the Year Round' well know the advantages of these readily prepared ingredients. But this is of no help to those who already have a clarifying problem.

As I mentioned before, isinglass and gelatine are tricky to handle and will have no effect upon starch or pectin hazes. Therefore we must look elsewhere. But if only, say, half a gallon is involved, you should first ask yourself: Is it worth going to a lot of trouble to get this clear, or shall I drink it as it is?

I suggest this because if the clouding is not heavy, the flavour of the wine is unlikely to be impaired to any great extent. But if the quantity is large or if friends are to be entertained with it, we must do something about it. And the first step is to find out whether starch or pectin is causing the trouble.

Pectin test

Take 1 fl oz of the wine and add 3 to 4 fl oz of methylated spirits. Shake well. If much pectin is present, jelly-like clots or strings will form almost immediately. If little pectin is present, some jellying will occur after about an hour. So keep the sample for a while if immediate clotting does not take place. If pectin is causing the trouble, a pectin-destroying enzyme must be employed – nothing else will do. When the pectin has been destroyed, the solids causing the clouding will join up and settle out.

Pectozyme is excellent for this purpose and is obtainable from any of the firms listed at the end of this book. 1 oz of Pectozyme will clarify about 15 gallons of wine. There are other proprietary named preparations which may be used if desired, and directions for their use will be given by the supplier. Bear in mind that, usually, 1 oz of these will clear up to 30 gallons.

The simplest means of treating wine with the pectin-destroying enzyme is this. Put the appropriate amount of enzyme in a very finely woven muslin bag or gathering of this material and suspend it in the wine. After a week, test the wine for clarity. If clarification has not taken place, leave it a bit longer. However, the wine usually becomes clear within a day or so, provided that it is kept in a warm place. But be careful not to let the wine become too warm, otherwise the enzyme may be destroyed. After clarification has occurred, rack the wine.

Starch test

As I mentioned before, starving the yeast of sugar in the early stages will often induce an enzyme in the yeast to convert starch into sugar. But this does not always happen so that starch causes the same kind of trouble as pectin. Root wines and those made with grains or apples are the offenders here.

To test for the presence of starch, take about 1 fl oz of the wine and add a few drops of tincture of iodine. The sample will turn dark blue or near black if starch is causing cloudiness in the wine. To test this reaction before using wine, you can see the effect if you drop a tiny amount of iodine on a slice of potato. Amylozyme 100 will clarify starch hazes. 1 oz should be sufficient for 4 to 5 gallons, depending on the amount of starch present. This enzyme may be used in exactly the same way as the pectin-destroying enzyme.

This takes care of the major problems which, as we have seen, should not arise if reliable methods are used. But what of hazes caused by neither pectin or starch? There are many proprietory clarifiers which will take care of these, and it would not be fair for me to recommend one against the other. All are reliable and all are supplied with directions for use.

However, if you want to try something quite handy, then egg-white should prove satisfactory. Up to eight gallons can be cleared with one egg-white. When using this it is best to put the wine in an open vessel, such as a fermentation vessel. Whisk the white of an egg to a stiff froth and mix it thoroughly with the wine. Return the wine to its jar. After clarification has taken place, rack in the normal way.

Filtering

I am amazed at the number of people who filter their wines almost as a matter of course, without even waiting to see whether they have a clearing problem or not. So let me say that filtering *should not* be necessary and will not improve the flavour of any wine. Nor will it remove cloudiness caused by the presence of pectin or starch.

However, as a last resort filtering may be used

where the amounts of wines are rather too small to use other clarifying agents satisfactorily. Asbestos pulp is undoubtedly very useful here, a quarter of a handful being sufficient for one gallon. Set aside a little of the wine to be treated and mix the pulp thoroughly with it. Put the pulp mixture back into the bulk of the wine and pour the whole lot through a jelly bag.

Set up a jar, complete with funnel, under the bag. But catch the first pint or so in a separate container and return it to the bag because it is likely to be cloudy. Only when you can see that the wine is coming through brilliant should you allow the wine into the jar. On no account press or squeeze the jelly bag otherwise you will get the opposite effect to the one you intended.

The main drawback with filtering is that it very often causes oxidation or over-oxidation. This is caused by long exposure to oxygen in the air, which the wine absorbs. A fully robust wine may lose much of its flavour after filtering, but it often recovers its former state after a period of time in store. However, delicate wines or those with, let's call them, 'tender' flavours, are likely to become quite flat and lifeless after filtering. They end up with none of the characteristics normally found in a wine. Beer is affected similarly. That occasional flat pint served over the bar is more often than not caused by oxidation.

There are modern means of avoiding this sort of thing, mainly by using various types of filters which have recently become available to home wine-makers. But this means a lot of expense for what is usually a very small quantity of wine, and I am the

last person to advise unnecessary expense. Far better
to avoid the causes that make filtering necessary. I
appreciate that most commercial wines are filtered,
but commercial producers treating perhaps a thous-
and gallons at a time use high-speed apparatus
which preclude the possibility of oxidation.

Siphoning

This is a very simple means of drawing wine from one container to another without disturbing the deposit, as would most certainly happen if the wine was poured instead. Many people shirk this operation because they think that there is some sort of mystery to it. There is no mystery, although it does fascinate many how the wine continues to flow. But what bothers many people is that they somehow break the siphon (stop the flow) and then clumsily stir up the deposit in getting it going again, thereby defeating the whole purpose of the operation.

Without siphoning wines from deposits, there would be no means of obtaining more than half a gallon of clear wine from a gallon jar. This would mean that the half gallon would have to be put into a suitably sized jar and allowed to clear. Even then you would be able to pour only about a quart of it before the sediment started to come over. Siphoning is infinitely more satisfactory because you are able to remove all but a quarter of an inch of wine from a jar without disturbing the deposit in any way.

Where most people go wrong when siphoning is that they forget that the bottom of the full jar (the jar to be siphoned) must be higher than the jar or bottle which is to receive the wine. It is therefore wise to arrange the full jar on a table or cupboard and the empty jar on the floor or on a stool. Provided that the top of the empty jar or bottle is at least an inch below the bottom of the full jar, all will be well.

If the full and empty jars were on the same level, nothing at all would happen. If the top of the empty jar were, say, half way up that of the full jar, only half the full jar would empty. This is because the flow would stop as the levels became equal.

Proper siphons with a squeeze bulb may be had at a price. But it is so simple to make an affective siphon for a few shillings that it is only common sense to make one for yourself. Almost any chemist will let you have a rubber bung with two holes in it – one in the centre and another near to it. With this you will need a glass tube about 16 to 17 inches long, one end of which has been turned up by about half an inch. Another glass tube to fit the second hole is also needed, and this need only be about 2 inches long. The bung must, of course, fit the jar it will be used with.

Fit the tubes in the bung as shown in the diagram, and attach a length of surgical rubber or non-toxic polythene tubing to the siphoning tube. This will slide on easily if it is wetted. Slip a stout rubber band over the glass and polythene tubing to hold them to each other firmly but without pinching the polythene tubing. This would hold up the flow. The polythene tubing should be 3 to $3\frac{1}{2}$ feet long. A siphon of these dimensions will be suitable for jars of up to three gallons. Fit the siphon into the jar, as shown in the diagram and suck gently at the free end of the polythene tubing until wine reaches your lips. Pinch the end of the tube tightly, put it into the jar or bottle, and allow the wine to flow. As the level in the bottle approaches the shoulder, pinch

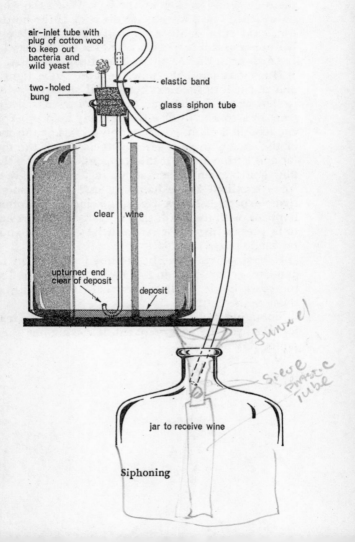

air-inlet tube with plug of cotton wool to keep out bacteria and wild yeast

two-holed bung

elastic band

glass siphon tube

clear wine

upturned end clear of deposit

deposit

funnel

sieve plastic tube

jar to receive wine

Siphoning

the tube gently to slow up the flow. When the wine has reached one-third way up the neck of the bottle, pinch the tube lightly to stop the flow completely. Do not stop the flow with a sudden jerk otherwise the deposit in the jar might be disturbed slightly.

Having stopped the flow, hold the tube tightly and put it into the next bottle and allow the wine to flow again. In this way, you can draw off all the wine in a continous flow without any hold up. You can lose the siphoning action only by raising the end of the tube above the level of the wine in the top jar and letting air in. If this happens, suck to get the flow going again. When siphoning, always have a spare sterilized bottle handy in case a little more than expected comes from the jar. This often happens, with the result that a vessel of any sort has to be pressed into service at a crucial stage. So do not be caught out.

Have your corks ready, sterilized as detailed in another section, and do not forget a spare one for the spare bottle. Write your labels before putting them on the bottles.

Siphoning and bottling operations can be a real joy when you are well prepared. If you are not, they can be very tedious.

Fermentation Cupboard

In other books I have recommended the use of a fermentation cupboard. But so many people seem at a loss to understand what is required, that I am including a few details here.

Almost any cupboard can be converted into a fermentation cupboard. The 'handy-carpenter-sort-of bloke' would have no trouble in making one to fit into a given space. About the only really important point is that the shelving should be of, say, $1\frac{1}{2}$ inch-wide strips of timber of suitable strength rather than ordinary shelving to allow for free circulation of warmth. They should be spaced about $1\frac{1}{2}$ inches apart.

The distance between the shelves should be the height of a jar and its fermentation lock with at least an inch to spare so that jars can be moved in and out without risk of knocking the locks to pieces on the shelf above. A cupboard with space for six one-gallon jars would allow you to make eighteen gallons a year, assuming that every gallon needed four months in the cupboard. Old kitchen cabinets, wardrobes or similar furniture would cost little to convert and would have quite a neat appearance.

One point, I think, should be brought home here. Do not make your cupboard according to the amount of wine you are making now. You may want to use two-gallon or three-gallon jars later on, so do allow for this. The illustration shows quite a small

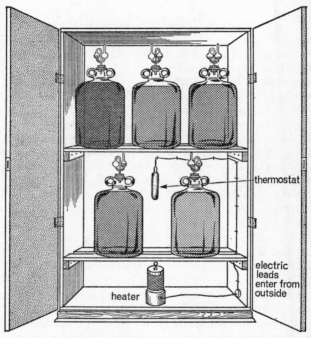

the cupboard may have either one or two doors to it

The Fermentation Cupboard

affair suitable for six jars. One jar has been left out of this to show the positioning of the thermostat.

If a taller cupboard is made for more jars, the thermostat should be hung half to two-thirds of the way up. A suitable heater known as the 100 W black heater, complete with thermostat already set at 70° F, is available from home-wine supplies for about 33s. I have been running one for many years and have not had to look at it since I installed it. As for the cost in power, I have noticed no increase in my electricity bills.

So do invest in a fermentation cupboard. You will soon find that your wine-making problems will iron themselves out. The constant temperature maintained by the cupboard assists enormously in the production of maximum alcohol and helps to prevent sticking ferments. Fermentation at a constant temperature is, as we have seen, important to quality wines. It also prevents these after-bottling blues when the corks blow out of bottles of wine which we thought had finished fermenting for good.

Sticking Ferments

What we mean by sticking ferments is that fermentation has 'stuck', i.e. that fermentation has stopped prematurely. In other words, it has stopped before the yeast can make the maximum alcohol possible.

When we make dry wines with less than $2\frac{1}{2}$ lb of sugar per gallon we cannot, of course, make the maximum alcohol because there is not enough sugar present to do this. But where we use more than $2\frac{1}{2}$ lb per gallon, the maximum alcohol should be made as a matter of course.

But it sometimes happens that fermentation 'sticks' when only, say, 11 to 12% of alcohol has been made. This occurrence is usually traced to a deficiency of some sort, lack of warmth, or over-heating. Unfortunately, it is not easy to track down the cause of a ferment sticking unless careful note is taken that sufficient nutrient, acid, tannin and other constituents have been added, and that the temperature has not gone up too high or been allowed to go too low.

Overheating will stop fermentation, and if it is decided that this is the cause, the best plan is to let the wine become quite cold for a few hours and to add fresh yeast. Then return the wine to its warm place. If you do this, fermentation should get going again within a few days, but it often takes a good deal longer. So leave it with a fermentation lock in place and be patient. Above all, do not worry.

When wine has stopped fermenting owing to cold, fermentation usually starts off again quite readily, although in obstinate cases it sometimes takes a week or ten days.

It is always wise to allow plenty of time for this important renewed fermentation to start again, as a full and complete fermentation is of the utmost importance to the quality and keeping qualities of the finished product.

Bothersome as these sticking ferments can sometimes be, they are all part of learning to make good wines. The more experienced you become, the less often this problem will arise. To bung down a wine that has ceased fermenting prematurely will only lead to the bungs blowing out at a later date, with all the consequential problems already discussed.

Difficulty in deciding when fermentation has ceased altogether and when it has merely stuck can be overcome by using the hydrometer habitually. Taking regular readings is not necessary. All you have to do is to take the reading before the yeast is added and record this on a label on the jar. If you add more sugar during the process, take the reading again before and after the addition, and again when fermenting ceases. The drops in readings are then added up so that you can tell whether the total drop has been 110° or not. If you look at Fermentation Chart No. 2, you will see at once how to do this.

If you do as many wine-makers do, despite all advice to the contrary, and add the sugar needed to make the alcohol they want and the sweetening sugar at the beginning, you will only have to take readings at the start and finish. For example, if you added sugar to give a reading of 1·110 to make the maximum alcohol and then added $4\frac{1}{2}$ oz of sugar to sweeten the wine, you would be starting with a gravity of 1·120 and should finish with 10° of sugar registering on the hydrometer when all fermentation has ceased. If the reading is higher than this, then fermentation has merely stuck, and every effort should be made to get it going again.

However, if there are only two or three degrees too much registering on the hydrometer, it is doubtful whether you will get fermentation going again. But it is worth leaving the wine in the warm under fermentation lock for a few weeks to see if it will. The fact that at this stage – when only two or three degrees have not been fermentated out – the particular yeast you used may have made all the alcohol it can. In this event, further fermentation is unlikely. Fresh yeast would not make any difference, because the percentage of alcohol present would most likely be enough to kill this fresh yeast instantly.

Unnecessary racking is very often the cause of fermenting ceasing prematurely. After the initial racking to rid the must of unwanted vegetable matter and dead yeast cells, it is wise to leave the wine undisturbed until all fermentation has ceased, unless a very heavy deposit builds up.

Lack of oxygen is another cause of sticking ferments. This is not to say that periodic airing of the must is necessary, but if fermentation is of rather longer than normal duration, removing the lock and replacing this with a knob of cotton wool for an hour is often advantageous.

Lack of organic matter and acid are other causes of sticking ferments. A well-balanced must, as I have already mentioned, is the answer to this aspect of the problem.

So, it all boils down to using a good recipe and a reliable method and keeping the wine warm during fermentation.

Balance of Acid

When we talk of balancing the acid content of a must, we mean correcting the amount of acid present to the amount desirable in the type of wine we are preparing. We may have to add some or we may have to take some out. It all depends on the type and ripeness of the fruit and the amount of acid it contains. A good summer will produce fruits lower in acid than those grown during a poor season. This alone is important. But even more important is the fact that different fruits contain widely differing amounts of acid. It is obvious then, that to obtain what is generally termed the correct acid balance is not an easy matter.

Indeed, this is the most difficult of all aspects of wine-making, and because I am committed to myself, my publishers and my vast readership to produce this book as the 'Simple' Science of Wine- and Beer-making, I am not going to recommend my readers to dabble in the use of acidimetric apparatus. This sort of thing is for the chemist or aspiring chemist who must also be a mathematician and certainly not for the average amateur working in his kitchen. Nevertheless, I am giving here a broad outline of what is involved when acidimetric apparatus is used. After this I explain a more simple means of obtaining a reasonable acid balance for the benefit of those who want to gain experience.

When producing wines, as most of us do, by

following recipes, there are bound to be some differences in the wines made from the same fruit and recipes. This is because of the differences in the climate from season to season; the differences in the type of soil and soil conditions; and the differences between the varieties of the same fruit. Even commercial producers with their own vines grown in the same soil cannot produce identical wines from year to year.

If commercial producers rely on the chemist to balance the must in every respect so that each constituent is balanced to the correct degree, then I am not surprised that some commercial wines taste as appetising as a paper mug of British Railways' coffee.

An excess or deficiency of acid in a finished wine does, of course, mean that some adjustment is necessary, but this can be done without resorting to the use of acidimetric apparatus (see 'Correcting Faults,' p. 83). When doing without this apparatus, we work in a somewhat clumsy fashion, but if the end product is satisfactory, it matters not how we get it.

Acidimetric apparatus is rather expensive and very fragile. The markings on it are in one-tenth of a millimetre. The apparatus includes a conical flask, for mixing the liquids and for observing the delicate colour changes, and a pipette, for measuring a precise amount of must. The pipette is a bulbous glass tube tapering to a point. Also included is a burette, which is used for measuring an exact amount of alkali. In addition, you need sodium hydroxide solution (alkali), distilled water, a weak solution of phenolphthalein (pronounced *fen-olf-thah-leen*), or other commercial colour indicators.

The object of using such apparatus is this. You take a certain quantity of your must, which contains acid, and add to it just enough alkali to neutralize the acid. You know when this point is reached by the change in colour of an indicator added with the must. By measuring the amount of alkali added, and knowing the strength of it, you can calculate how much acid is present in your sample of must and hence in the bulk. The procedure is as follows:

Suck a small sample of must into the pipette. Rinse out the pipette with this and discard the sample. Draw in a further sample and, by using pressure from a finger, transfer a given amount of must to the flask. The amount will vary according to the size of the operation. This operation requires some practice if it is to be accurate. Bear in mind that when working to one-tenth of a millimetre, even a very tiny inaccuracy can cause a calamitous error in the overall effect of the experiment. Then add phenolphthalein and distilled water to the flask in appropriate amounts.

Rinse out the burette with sodium hydroxide solution and discard the sample. Fill the burette again to the level indicated. Allow this solution to drip into the flask by opening the tiny screw-up tap at the bottom of the burette. Carry on until the mixture in the flask just changes colour. This is easy to discern when musts or wines have little colour of their own, but red wines or musts are a very different matter. Take the reading on the burette. The difference between the initial and final readings gives you the volume of alkali used to neutralize the acid in the sample of must.

From here the mathematician takes over to calculate the answer to our experiment from a formula that says that the volume of alkali used (V_1) multiplied by the normality (strength) of the alkali (N_1) is equal to the volume of acid present (V_2) multiplied by the normality of the acid (N_2). The calculation on paper would appear like this:

$$V_1 \times N_1 = V_2 \times N_2$$

Since we know V_1, N_1 and V_2, we can calculate N_1 – the strength of acid.

Having come this far, I am sure you will all agree that it is time we turned to something more simple. Using narrow-range indicator papers is more in line with an amateur's requirements. Those who use them usually begin with a recipe and test the must after it has been prepared. If adjustment is necessary, it can be made without much bother.

Most of you will already know and understand that a percentage of acid is absolutely necessary not only for the fullness and flavour of a finished wine but also from the point of view of a satisfactory fermentation.

Recipes for wines made from ingredients that contain little or no acid – such as dried fruit, flowers and roots – always include oranges, lemons or both, or the equivalent in citric or tartaric acid, in order to have a reasonable amount of acid in the must and in the finished wine. The resulting wine is usually good, but a good few amateurs like to adjust the acid content when these ingredients are used.

Recipes for fruits are different in that they are usually evolved with the acid content of the fruit taken into account. Thus we have recipes calling for so many pounds of fruit per gallon of water. The weight of the fruit is related to the amount of acid it contains.

If a good deal of fruit is used, then it stands to reason that much more acid will be present in the must and therefore in the finished wine. The same applies when some unripe fruits are used. This is obviously the reason for so many people sticking faithfully to reliable recipes.

Now let us see what an acid solution (prepared must) amounts to without becoming too technical. First of all, water is a neutral solution. This is because the positively charged hydrogen ions are exactly balanced by negatively charged hydroxyl ions. Water, therefore, is neither acid nor alkaline. But add a little acid to the water and you at once increase its hydrogen-ion content so that it becomes an acid solution.

In fruit juices and musts prepared from fruits, the hydrogen ions are always in excess, and those who want to balance their must will have to find out just what this excess amounts to. What is known as the 'pH value' is merely a number used to indicate the concentration of hydrogen ions present, and the range is pH 7 – a neutral solution – to pH 0 – extreme acidity.

It is usual to aim for pH 3, but a lot depends on personal requirements. A set of British Drug Houses' narrow-range indicator papers can be obtained, together with a colour chart. You will need the one covering the range pH 2·5 to pH 4·0. To test the acid content, you merely dip the paper into a prepared must. The paper will change colour according to the amount of acid present. Compare the colour with the colour chart, which shows the pH value of each colour.

If you have to increase the acid to the pH value you want, add acid either in the form of citric acid from a chemist or lemon juice (which is the same thing) a drop at a time, testing at intervals. P.L.J. is very useful for this, too. On the other hand, if too much acid is present, some will have to be removed, and this can be done easily enough by adding pure medicinal (precipitated) chalk. Alternatively, you can add water to a fully flavoured must in order to dilute the acid to the pH required.

Precipitated chalk is the stuff you pay dearly for when you buy an antacid at the chemist's. The action of the chalk in a must or in a wine is the same as that of an antacid used to settle an upset stomach. The chalk reacts with the acid so that it settles out. After treating a wine with chalk, you can see sparkling crystals in the sediment that settles out.

Using the chalk

The amount to use is a matter of absolute trial and error. But before using any at all it is wise to ponder for a moment whether the amount of acid is really too much or not. Your palate will guide you on this. If after testing, the amount is only very slightly above what you really need, there is hardly any point in altering it. If you do decide to use chalk you can get it from a chemist for about 4d an ounce. Rather than treat the whole of the must, it is a good plan to treat about a pint of it. Take a little of the sample and stir in a teaspoonful of chalk. Then mix this with the remainder. Let it stand for a few hours until the chalk has settled out.

The sample will then be free from acid. Return it to the bulk without letting any of the chalk deposit come over. If you have prepared a gallon of must, you will, when adding the acid-free pint, dilute the acid in the bulk by one-eighth. This is a far more sensible way of doing it rather than treating the whole of the bulk because it reduces the risk of taking out too much. Further sample pints may be treated if necessary. Testing with test papers at intervals will show how you are progressing.

Since this is all very simple, any amateur wanting to experiment, if only for the sake of obtaining practical experience, will find it very interesting. Those who really do want to try their hand at balancing the acid in a must will find this method very easy to get along with.

Naturally, you will have your doubts to begin with, but practical experience will give you confidence so that, if balancing a must is going to be the normal practice, it will quickly become second nature to do it. More about the use of precipitated chalk appears under 'Correcting Faults', p. 84.

Maturing, Storage Problems and Preserving

MATURING

There is no doubt that maturing is the final phase in the production of quality wines. And alas, it is true that a multitude of amateur wine-makers never let their wines prove themselves. Many of them think: 'This wine tastes all right as it is, I can't see it improving all that much. So here goes' – and, hey presto, it has gone almost before the next batch is in the fermenting vessel. But if they would put away even one bottle and taste it in a year or two, how they would kick themselves for drinking the rest so young.

Such vast differences are found between young and old wines that it is not unrealistic to liken young wines to boisterous, ill-mannered children and old wines to gentle old folk with lovable dispositions. Despite this, young wines are often quite good and worth drinking as they are, but they improve very gradually over a couple of years. Generally young wines are quite rough and sharp to the palate with nothing really to recommend them other than promise of better things to come. Some, in fact, are so 'disappointing' that I have known people to think that they have gone wrong in one way or another.

When, years ago, we formed a wine-making circle

in the area in which I live, one member actually brought a gallon along to ask my opinion. It had ceased fermenting a few weeks earlier. It was quite brilliant, but was rough and lacked bouquet. Although the flavour was not as good as it should have been for the type of wine, I knew that all it needed was a couple of years to settle down. I could not really find fault with such young wine. When I told this member to keep it for a couple of years because it would improve beyond all recognition he, like most disbelieving beginners, simply would not be convinced. He would have none of it, thinking as many do that I was just kidding him. Honestly, I often wonder whether people like that want to learn or not.

Anyway, he told me that he wanted the jar for another batch and, if I liked it, I could take it and let him have the jar at the next meeting. This I did because I knew it was useless to argue with one who had already made up his mind. It was about two years later when I took along a bottle as my sample for the evening. The member who gave me that gallon was there as usual. When his turn came to taste my wine he went into raptures over it, even offering to buy a couple of bottles for Christmas if I had them to spare. I had to confess that I had only five bottles because he had given me a gallon! He was dumbfounded.

All young wines must be given time to develop – except perhaps the very driest, which rarely improve after a year unless they are very rough. Others really ought to be given two years at least. I realize that this is a very long time for those anxious to drink their wines because they have nothing to drink for two or three years from the time they start out. The easiest way out of this problem is to make a large amount of suitable varieties and, while some can be drunk young, the larger part of each batch can be allowed to mature. In this way, although you will be drinking immature and therefore inferior wines, you will at least have something while the rest is improving.

How to store the maturing wines is a matter not very easily solved because most amateurs rarely make sufficient of the one sort to fill a barrel. But those who do make amounts of five and ten gallons really ought to consider storing them in four-and-a-half gallon or nine-gallon barrels.

It is during storage in wooden containers of this sort that oxygen percolates through the pores of the wood in very tiny but beneficial amounts to cause much desired oxidation. This, it must be understood, is certainly different to the over-oxidation that can take place when the whole of the wine is exposed to air, say, when filtering.

When in barrels, chemical changes and reactions are constantly taking place. Some run with each other, or concurrently, while others depend on the one before, and therefore run consecutively. All that takes place is very far from being understood. But we do know that maturing really means the marrying, or shall we call it the interweaving, of the many constituents that go to make up a wine.

Flavours are improved by chemical action, while esters develop to produce a bouquet. But these processes would be interrupted and the result hindered if unnecessary racking or other disturbances were allowed. Therefore, wines put away in bulk should

E

not be disturbed – not even moved from one place to another – if it is at all possible to avoid doing so.

Time is the important factor because maturing should always be slow. In fact, you are unlikely to be able to hurry it. Deciding just when a wine is mature is probably the hardest part of wine-making. And I doubt whether anybody could hope to decide for you when wines have matured sufficiently in bulk to be bottled to finish maturing. This is something peculiar to each wine, probably because each contains a varying amount of chemical matter and other constituents which have to undergo certain changes. Therefore, a wine containing more of each constituent will doubtless take longer to mature than a wine containing less. Certainly, with the minute amount of oxygen percolating through the pores of the wood, these changes take place more quickly than when the wine is stored in stone or glass jars when the oxygen can percolate only through the bung.

This is not to say that maturing is too quick when storing in barrels or that it is too slow when storing in jars. If slow maturing is best, then it would seem that jars – with only the bung to let oxygen through – would be ideal. But this is not so. Rather too little oxygen can get in through the bung.

The fact is that wood is best for maturing not only from the point of view of oxygen ingress but also for another reason. The wine absorbs beneficial substances from the wood, while the wood in turn absorbs a certain amount of harshness or perhaps tartness from the wine. Do not think that wood will absorb too much of some constituent because it will not.

Even so, there comes a time when the wine should not be left in the wood any longer, simply because there is a risk of over-oxidation. This is the time when the wine has reached the point where sufficient oxidation has taken place and when the wine should be bottled to finish maturing. In the bottle important changes continue to take place. As I have mentioned, these are not fully understood, which is the professional way of saying that the process is still almost a complete mystery. When wines are bottled and sealed, further oxidation cannot take place, and the further chemical action, reaction and inter-action, and the marrying of constituents can go on without risk of over-oxidation.

It is not possible for anybody to lay down hard and fast rules, or for that matter even hazard a guess as to when sufficient oxidation has taken place. Only the person who made the wine can judge, and he can only do this by tasting.

Tasting at this stage should show that the wine has mellowed and become much smoother and more wholesome. In fact, there should be a very notice-able change in the quality compared with that when the wine was first stored. And here it must rest with the individual as to when sufficient maturing in wood has taken place. Lighter wines usually mature more quickly than the heavier sorts. But neither develops much in the way of aroma or bouquet while in the wood, so do not expect this. As a rough guide, wines should be mellowed in wood for a year and then allowed to mature in bottle for a further year.

In bottle, chemical action and reaction continue. Even though this is not fully understood, it is reasonable to suppose that chemical interaction is responsible for the changes which produce aromatic, volatile esters which add markedly to the aroma and bouquet of the wine. It is doubtful whether this would happen in the presence of oxygen, and it is therefore while stored in bottle that greater changes take place. But whether the changes would take place successfully if wines were not allowed a mellowing period in the wood is another matter. It seems to me that, for the best results, the success of the improvement in bottle depends very much on the effectiveness of the period in the wood. But what of those who cannot use wooden containers for the early stages? Jars and ordinary bungs must be used and, as we have seen, the area of the bung allows for very little percolation of oxygen. This means that under these circumstances the first stage of maturing is likely to take a good deal longer than is desired. I think that this must be the reason for those jars of our grandparents' day that had bung-holes three or four inches in diameter. These would certainly be more advantageous from the maturing point of view when jars must be used. Today, most jars have bung-holes hardly more than an inch and a half in diameter. So be it, we have to use them.

A certain amount of aeration could be affected by lifting the bung and replacing this with a firm knob of cotton wool for a few minutes every three months or so. If this is tried, the area around the bung and the bung itself must be well washed with sterilizing solution prior to removal. And, although jars of wine are usually stored in inaccessible places, it is best to do this without moving the jar, no matter how difficult this might be. I say this because I am convinced that one of the most important factors concerning successful maturing is non-disturbance.

STORING

Temperature and darkness are two very important factors here. There is very little the average amateur can do about storing in the ideal temperature simply because he has to store wherever he can. But it is worthwhile during the maturing period to attempt to keep the temperature fairly constant at around 50° F. This is impossible for most people who have to store in outhouses, cellars or under the stairs. But where central heating and a spare room are available, this should not prove too difficult.

Darkness is very important to most wines. Those stored in stone jars or in wood present no problem, but those stored in glass jars or plastic containers which admit light, must be kept in the dark, the affect of light is quite often disastrous. Direct light can quickly and irreparably ruin colour, flavour, and bouquet, so that the wines simply are not *worth a second tasting*. Containers that admit light must therefore be kept in the dark. This is not to say that occasional opening of a door that admits light to the storage area would have harmful effect; it would not. But prolonged exposure to moderate light certainly would.

Red wines are particularly susceptible to the effect of light; hence the need to store in the dark and in dark glass bottles – it does not matter if they be dark brown or dark green. But clear or semi-clear glass should never be used. The paler coloured wines to the true whites seem unharmed by light, but I always take the precaution never to expose them unnecessarily. Pale reds to pink wines should also be put into dark glass bottles.

It is during storage that many beginners (and plenty with experience as well) come up against one big problem — that of re-fermentation. Yet this is a problem that should never arise. What usually happens is that the wine-maker discovers, much to his consternation, that a bung is missing from a jar. It may have popped out five minutes or a month earlier. Very often the wine is exposed to air for long periods without him knowing it. The result is that over-oxidation takes place or that the wine is attacked by wild yeasts or bacteria. Nearly always the wine is spoiled if exposure of this sort is prolonged.

It sometimes happens, when breaking the seal of a bottle, that the cork blows out and the wine fizzes up like champagne. Usually it is cloudy and tastes awful. The simple explanation for this occurrence and for blown bungs is that fermentation was not complete when the wine was put in store.

Many, many wine-makers experience this and are dismayed simply because they think the wine, which was quite good when put away, has gone wrong. Nothing has gone seriously wrong unless the wine has been spoilt owing to exposure to air or to attack by yeast or bacteria. This depends on how long the bung has been missing. In the case of bottled products, re-fermenting in this fashion does no harm other than make the wine become cloudy.

When the bung blows from a jar, a fermentation lock must be fitted and the jar brought into the warm where it must remain until all renewed fermentation has ceased. When bottled products re-ferment, the remainder of the batch must first be tracked down. Then the whole lot must be returned to a jar with a fermentation lock fitted and left in the warm.

The trouble in both cases is that fermentation stopped prematurely, most likely owing to cold in late autumn or early winter (see 'Sticking Ferments', p. 112). This often happens when warmth is not given. The fermenting must becomes cold and causes the yeast to go dormant when, say, only 10 to 12% of alcohol has been made.

Later, when the warmth of spring penetrates to the wine, the yeast becomes active again. So all that is really happening is that fermentation is merely continuing from where it left off. This can be a confounded nuisance and a blessing in disguise at the same time. Always bear in mind that, provided spoilage yeasts or bacteria have not attacked the wine while the bung was missing, you will get a far better wine after this renewed fermentation.

Renewed fermentation is much easier to avoid – and can be prevented altogether – by using a fermentation cupboard.

PRESERVING

It should be made clear at once that there should be no need to preserve well-made wines containing the maximum amount of alcohol. This is because there should be sufficient alcohol in the wine to preserve it.

However, it does sometimes happen that, despite having good yeasts and having had a thoroughly good fermentation, the maximum alcohol is not made. It could be that you have missed the mark by as little as one per cent. This may leave the wine less capable of combating disease, but it may also leave the yeast in a position to recommence fermenting – as we have just discussed.

Obviously, before we go to the trouble of preserving wines, it is as well to find out whether they are stable or not. If they are stable, then preserving is not necessary. But if, after the normal processes of fermentation, it is discovered that a wine is not stable, then preserving should be carried out. Either way, nothing in this line should be done until all fermentation has ceased in the normal way or until you are satisfied that the wine is a finished product ready to be put away to mature. Then, and only then, should the test be carried out to find whether the wine is stable or not. Users of the hydrometer should be able to verify whether they have made the maximum alcohol, so there should be no doubts for them. Even so, they may carry out the following simple test if only from the point of view of interest and practical experience.

Test for Stability

Almost every chemist will let you have cheaply two small test-tubes with a rubber or cork stopper for one of them. Or perhaps firms dealing in home wine-making equipment retail these now – they used not to. Two small aspirin or other very small bottles will do if nothing else is available. Thoroughly sterilize and rinse the tubes or bottles and shake them free of as much water as you can. Dry thoroughly, otherwise one or two drops of water will dilute the sample and give an inaccurate reaction.

Half-fill both vessels with the wines to be tested.

Cork and seal one tightly. Cut a small piece of flat, stiff card to a little larger than the top of the second container and rest this on the top of it. Stand the samples side by side in a warm room for twenty-four hours. If both samples are exactly the same colour after this then the wine is stable and need not be preserved. On the other hand, if the unsealed sample has turned a darker colour, the wine is unstable and should be preserved.

Dry Wines

Thoroughly fermented out, bone-dry wines, made with less sugar than produces the maximum alcohol, are another matter. All bone-dry wines are better for having a lower-than-average alcohol content, although many people make them to contain the maximum. But when they have been made to contain less than 14% of alcohol by volume, preserving should be carried out. This is not because they are likely to ferment again. They cannot do this simply because there is no unfermented sugar left. But there is alway a risk of the acetic change taking place unless they are preserved.

This is not to say that the acetic change is automatic or even likely, but it can happen. The risk comes during siphoning or otherwise racking, when these wines are exposed to the risk of contamination by the acetic bacteria. Bear in mind that the weaker the wine, the more susceptible it is to disease. On the whole, if bone-dry wines are handled carefully throughout and kept in containers which are full, there should be no risk whatsoever. However, these wines will not travel. In other words, they will not

stand being moved about a lot unless they are preserved.

Preserving

Chemical preservation is undoubtedly the cheap-
est and most reliable method. This is practised by
the trade on a far wider scale than is generally
imagined. Almost all wines are preserved. The
low-alcohol wines are preserved chemically, while
the higher-alcohol ones, such as sherries and ports,
are fortified (strengthened) with added alcohol.
If this were not the case, there would be no high-
alcohol wines simply because the trade cannot produce more alcohol in their wines by the normal
processes of fermentation than we amateurs can,
except perhaps by as little as one or two per cent.

Sherries have spirit added at the end of fermentation, but port and a good many other wines have
it added quite early in the process. When port, for
example, is being fermented, skilled tasters sample
by taste and by testing apparatus to ascertain the
amount of sugar used up, the strength of flavour,
the general sweetness to the palate, and so on. When
all these things are satisfactory, large amounts of
spirit are added. This kills the yeast and therefore
halts fermentation, and at the same time fortifies the
wine to the percentage of alcohol required.

That is why the high-alcohol wines are so robust,
so full of flavour and have such wonderful aroma
and bouquet. Only the natural sugar in the grapes
has been fermented, whereas we have to add sugar
to produce the amount of alcohol we want. And for
this we must use cane sugar. The trade have no need

to do this for they utilize only a certain amount of the sugar the grapes contain. The rest is left un-fermented. The added alcohol brings out the flavour and bouquet to the full. The added alcohol is what we pay for in the more expensive wines. The cheaper sorts, being preserved chemically, cost far less to produce.

Campden tablets are used for chemical preserva-tion, and it is quite a simple matter to treat any amount of wine, however large or small, in this way. A well-made wine with a good percentage of alcohol, but one shown to be unstable by the test already mentioned, should not need more than one Camp-den tablet to each gallon. Crush this to powder in a small cup or glass with something not metal, such as the handle of a wooden spoon. Mix a little wine with it and stir the sample into the bulk. Cork the jar for twenty-four hours and repeat the test des-cribed earlier. You will know from this test whether or not a further tablet is necessary.

Two tablets are usually the maximum needed. Indeed, where delicately flavoured wines are pre-served in this fashion, more than one tablet would be likely to affect the flavour. Wines with a full flavour would not be affected by a little more. But even with these, where two tablets have been used and more than one needed, the next addition should be half a tablet. When preserving in this fashion we are using the permitted preservative of sulphur dioxide. The amount allowed by law in wines in this country is 450 parts of preservative to 1,000,000 parts wine. This amount is represented by eight Campden tablets. From this we see that, in using two or even three tablets, we are well within the safety limits.

It is often with the sweet wines that more than two tablets are needed, especially if their alcohol content is low. This is because they are very liable to re-fermentation and very susceptible to disease. It is always best, therefore, to strive to make the maximum alcohol when making sweet wines, unless, of course, you like low-alcohol sweet wines. In this case, make them and then preserve.

Preserving with Spirit

As mentioned, the higher-alcohol wines such as port are fortified during the process of fermentation not only to preserve them but also to retain their natural sugar content, to enhance their bouquet, and to increase their alcohol content. This sort of thing is beyond the reach of the amateur because it is very expensive.

However, we are able to increase the alcohol content by an important two or three per cent at not too great expense when we have turned out exceptional wines worth preserving for themselves and for keeping for many years. The addition of spirit will also bring about important improvements in aroma and bouquet during storage.

The trade use a number of brandies for this purpose, some of which are produced from the residue of a batch of perhaps thousands of gallons of wine – an enormous cake of skins and pips left after the wine has been drawn off. This cake is treated with water and allowed to ferment further. The resulting very poor wine, which has rather a low percentage of alcohol, is then distilled. Certain flavours and esters are allowed to come over during distillation so that this brandy has a flavour that makes it suitable for adding to a certain type of wine. But many brandies are produced which are quite neutral in both flavour and colour. This characteristic is often produced only by filtering the finished product through charcoal. When we talk of brandies, we immediately think of world-famous names, but almost all spirits distilled by the wine trade for fortification purposes are known as brandies.

It is with brandies quite neutral in both flavour and colour that we are likely to be interested. This is because when preserving wines we do not want to alter the colour or flavour of them. Rums, tradenamed brandies such as the cognacs, whiskies and gins will all flavour wines and, in most cases, spoil them. Imagine a well-made blackberry or elderberry wine with a hint of the flavour of rum, or even brandy for that matter. It would be quite out of character with the rest of the wine. It would be rather like taking good coffee and then detecting the taste of tea as you swallow it.

When fortifying or preserving, it is almost always best to use a spirit with neither colour or flavour. For this purpose, two grades of spirits are available – Polish pure spirit at 140° proof and Vodka at 70° proof.

Before we go any further I think it is necessary to explain the difference between alcohol by volume and proof spirit, how these are compared with each other, and just what 'proof' means. This will clarify what is often one of the biggest mysteries confronting the average amateur.

When we refer to alcohol by volume, whether it

be the amount in fifty gallons, one gallon, one bottle or half a glass, the percentage is the number of volumes of pure alcohol in each one hundred volumes of wine. Therefore, if we have half a glass of wine of 14% of alcohol by volume, we have fourteen volumes of pure alcohol in each hundred volumes. To put it another way, one hundred gallons of the wine will contain fourteen gallons of pure alcohol.

The term 'proof' is a relic of ancient times when there was no accurate means of measuring the amount of alcohol present in liquors. Hence the confusion these days when accuracy is essential.

A liquor that is 100° proof spirit actually contains only 57% by volume – which is just over half of what the average person might imagine it to be. Gin of 70° proof has the more accurate corresponding figure of 40% by volume. A spirit of 175° proof is actually 100% by volume – pure alcohol. The following table may be useful. This does not cover the whole range as this is not necessary. But it does cover the range which most amateurs may find useful for reference purposes from time to time.

Relation between alcohol by volume and proof spirit

% Alcohol by volume	° Proof spirit
10	17·5
12	21
14	24·5
16	28
18	31·5
20	35
22	42·1
24	39
26	46
28	49·2
30	52·5
35	61·3
40	70

When preserving with spirit, it is not necessary to add large amounts as all most of us want is to increase the alcohol content from the average of 14% by volume (24·5° proof) to about 16% by volume (28° proof). Indeed, this is all that is necessary for preservation purposes. You can, of course, increase the percentage further if you want to.

In the following tables, which show how much of various spirits to add to obtain a given percentage of alcohol, it is presumed that your wine contains 14% by volume. Any well-made wine should contain this amount.

Here it is important to use the type of bottle relating to the table involved. British standard wine bottles and those containing gin and whisky – full-size bottles that is – hold 26 fl oz when filled to the usual level. Whereas many bottles, especially those from Continental countries, hold one pint – 20 fl oz or a fraction more according to the type of bottle. Those tall bottles without shoulders are the sort that usually hold a pint. To be on the safe side and to make your fortifying effective and inexpensive, it would be as well to fill a doubtful bottle to the usual level with water and then pour the water into a measuring jug.

The tables are designed for fortifying one bottle at a time as this is the most that the average winemaker will want to start with. The best means of adding the spirit is to put it into an empty bottle and fill up with wine. To find the degrees proof corresponding to the per cent by volume given in these tables, see the table 'Relation between Alcohol by Volume and Proof Spirit' on page 138.

Fortification Table 1
Using Vodka to produce a one pint bottle (20 fl oz)
of fortified wine

Add these fl oz of Vodka	*To these fl oz of wine of 14%*	*% Alcohol by volume in the fortified wine*
FOR A 1-PINT BOTTLE (20 FL OZ)		
1	19	15·3
2	18	16·6
3	17	17·9
4	16	19·2
5	15	20·5
FOR A STANDARD BRITISH WINE BOTTLE (26 FL OZ)		
1	25	15
2	24	16
3	23	17
4	22	18
5	21	19

Using Vodka, as in the foregoing table, is convenient. Provided that the wines so treated have full flavour, the amounts of Vodka added are unlikely to dilute the flavour to any noticeable extent. However, this would not be true for wines with a delicate flavour. These include wines made from flowers or other ingredients that do not give such robust flavour as most English wild and garden fruits.

Where rather milder-flavoured wines are to be treated, and especially where more than 2 fl oz of Vodka would be needed, some dilution of flavour is bound to result. It is therefore advisable to use a stronger spirit so that less is needed to do the job. The cost is the same whichever you use. Fortification Table No. 2 is for using Polish pure spirit, which is obtainable from the suppliers listed at the end of the book.

Fortification Table 2
Using Polish pure spirit of 140% proof (80% by Volume)
to produce a bottle of fortified wine

Add these fl oz of spirit	To these fl oz of wine of 14%	% Alcohol by volume in the fortified wine
FOR A 1-PINT BOTTLE (20 FL OZ)		
1	19	17·3
2	18	20·6
3	17	23·9
FOR A STANDARD BRITISH WINE BOTTLE (26 FL OZ)		
1	25	16·5
2	24	19·1
3	23	21·6
4	22	24·2

F

A Selection of Recipes

INTRODUCTION

The number of recipes here cannot possibly be as numerous as in my other books because most of the space here is occupied by the simple science and chemistry of the subject. However, the selection is wide and varied so that every reader will be able to find several recipes that will suit him nicely.

The recipes and methods are simplicity itself. The aim now should be to select a recipe that will make the type (sweet or dry) and variety of wine you most like. As this passes through the various stages of production, you may re-read the details appertaining to each stage so that you understand what is going on. Sterilization of the must is all part of the methods detailed, but sterilization of utensils, and so on, must be carried out as required.

Whether you test for acidity and balance this and whether you use the hydrometer or not is entirely a matter for you to decide. However, I do hope you will do this (unless it is your first attempt at winemaking) to obtain more accurate results and make your wine-making far more interesting. Bear in mind that the practical experience gained from doing this sort of thing is always valuable.

Bear in mind also that when we imitate certain commercial products we only imitate – we cannot turn them out *identical* to commercial wines. Nevertheless, as your experience grows and you learn to vary the ingredients to obtain special results, you will make wines very close to the commercial product you are imitating. It is important to remember, though, that each batch of wine you make using the same recipe, method, and ingredients, will vary slightly from the others.

No book on this subject would be complete without recipes and methods for making wines from garden and wild fruits. These will always be popular despite the fact that there is an abundance of ready-to-use ingredients available today. When using garden and wild fruits I have, wherever possible, included the making of more than one type of wine from the basic ingredient in order to give you a wide choice. A small number of recipes for making wines with ready-to-use ingredients appear under their own heading.

It will be found that my recipes do not produce an initial must with a specific gravity of 1·110. This is because for the sake of simplicity and to ensure that the specific gravity is not higher than the figure quoted, I advocate adding half the sugar at the start and half later in the process. Those wishing to start off with a certain specific gravity will find it quite simple to achieve after studying the relevant chapter.

Wines from Garden and Wild Fruits

IMITATION DUBONNET

For ordinary elderberry wine, ignore the use of essence of cinchona bark.

3 lb elderberries · essence of cinchona bark
3 lb sugar for sweet (2½ lb for dry, and imitation
Dubonnet) · yeast · nutrient · 1 gallon water

Put the elderberries in a fermenting vessel and crush well by hand. Pour on 2 pints of water. Crush and dissolve 1 Campden tablet in a little warm water and stir this into mixture. Leave covered for a few hours.

Meanwhile, boil half the sugar to be used in 4 pints of water for 2 minutes. When cool add to the fruit, and give it a thorough stirring. Add yeast and nutrient, cover, and ferment in a warm place for 6 to 7 days (8 or 9 days if making imitation Dubonnet – this is to produce slightly more natural tannin). Each day, stir gently and cover again at once.

After the prescribed time, strain out the solids, wring the pulp fairly dry and return the strained wine to the (cleaned) fermenting vessel. Boil the remaining sugar in 1 pint of water for 2 minutes and, when cool, add to the vessel. Cover again as before and ferment for a further 3 to 4 days. Then transfer to a jar, and fit a fermentation lock. Leave until all fermentation has ceased.

As this is doubtless your first attempt at imitating Dubonnet, it is wise to leave the addition of cinchona essence until the wine is a finished product. Some people like more than others, so until you know from experience how much to add, it is wise to treat one bottle at a time by adding one drop at a time.

IMITATION BEAUJOLAIS

2 lb blackberries · 2 lb elderberries · 2¼ lb sugar
yeast · nutrient · approx. 1 gallon water

Put the two fruits in a fermenting vessel and crush
well by hand. Crush and dissolve 1 Campden tablet
in a little warm water and stir this into the mixture.
Leave covered for a few hours. Meanwhile boil half
the sugar to be used in 4 pints of water for 2
minutes and, when cool, thoroughly stir it into the
fruit. Add yeast and nutrient, cover, and leave to
ferment for 7 to 8 days, stir daily.

After this time, strain out the solids, squeeze the
pulp fairly dry, and return the strained wine to
the cleaned fermenting vessel. Leave to ferment,
covered as before, for 3 to 4 more days. Then pour
carefully into a jar, leaving as much deposit behind
as you can. Boil the remaining sugar in 2 pints of
water for 2 minutes and, when cool, add to the jar.
Then fit a fermentation lock and leave until all
fermentation has ceased.

BLACKBERRY WINE

3–4 lb blackberries · 3 lb sugar for sweet, (2½ lb
sugar for dry) · yeast nutrient · approx. 1 gallon
water

Use the method for imitation Beaujolais – omitting
the elderberries.

IMITATION SAUTERNES

The characteristic flavour of Sauternes is produced
by a mould peculiar to the variety of grape used,

and because we do not have these grapes, it follows that we cannot produce this mould. The grapes used in this recipe must be in good condition and be of a reasonably sweet variety. Outdoor grapes will do provided they are fully ripe.

5 lb green grapes · 5 lb apples (dessert sweet)
2 lb sugar · yeast · nutrient · water as in method

In this recipe I have estimated that you will obtain a total of 12 oz sugar from the ingredients making a total of 2 lb 12 oz sugar, which should be just about right for the type of wine. Users of the hydrometer may vary the amount of sugar according to whim. The actual amount of sugar produced by the ingredients will depend entirely on variety and stage of ripeness.

Crush the grapes by hand and put them in a fermenting vessel. Pour on 2 pints of water. Crush and dissolve 1 Campden tablet in a little warm water and stir this into the mixture. Cover and leave for a few hours. Meanwhile, boil half the sugar to be used in 2 pints water for 2 minutes and, when cool, add to the grapes and stir thoroughly.

Peel and core the apples and chop very finely or mince them. Add 1 pint of water and treat with a Campden tablet as for the grapes. Leave for an hour, then stir thoroughly and mix with the grapes. Add yeast and nutrient, and ferment in a warm place for 8 to 9 days, stirring daily, and pressing the apple pulp as much as possible.

After this time, strain out solids and squeeze as dry as possible. Return the strained wine to the (cleaned) fermenting vessel. Boil the remaining sugar in 2 pints of water for 2 minutes and, when cool, add to the vessel. Cover and ferment for a further 3 to 4 days. Then transfer to a jar, leaving as much deposit behind as you can. Fit a fermentation lock and leave until all fermentation has ceased.

BLACKCURRANT WINES

An excellent sweet wine
4 lb blackcurrants · 3 lb sugar · yeast · nutrient
water as in method

An excellent dry wine
2½ lb blackcurrants · 2¼ lb sugar · yeast · nutrient
water as in method

Crush the fruit by hand in a fermenting vessel and pour on 4 pints of water. Crush and dissolve 1 Campden tablet in a little warm water and stir this into the mixture. Leave for a few hours. Meanwhile, boil half the sugar to be used in 2 pints of water for 2 minutes and when cool add to the fruit and stir thoroughly. Add yeast and nutrient and ferment for 8 to 9 days.

After this time, strain and wring out as dry as possible and return the strained wine to the (cleaned) fermenting vessel.

Boil the remaining sugar in 1 pint water and when cool add to the rest. Leave to ferment for a further 3 to 4 days. Then transfer to a jar, fit a fermentation lock, and leave until all fermentation has ceased.

IMITATION RIESLING

Riesling is not to my liking, but many people find it delightful. This recipe should give a good imitation.

5 lb apples · 1 lb rhubarb · 1 lb sultanas · 2 lb sugar
yeast · nutrient · water as in method

Core the apples and remove stalks, but do not peel. Remove any blemishes. Mince or chop finely the apples and the sultanas. Crush the rhubarb with a rolling pin. Put the crushed fruit in a fermenting vessel with 4 pints of water.

Crush and dissolve 2 Campden tablets in a little water and stir this into the mixture. (2 tablets because of the larger-than-average bulk.) Boil half the sugar to be used in 2 pints of water for 2 minutes and, when cool, add to the mixture, giving it a very vigorous stirring for a minute or so.

Add yeast and nutrient and ferment in a warm place for 7 to 8 days, stirring daily. After this time, strain out the solids and press them as dry as possible. Return the strained wine to the (cleaned) fermenting vessel and leave to ferment for a further 5 to 6 days.

Then pour carefully into a jar leaving as much deposit behind as you can. Boil the remaining sugar in ½ pint of water for 2 minutes and, when cool, add to the jar. Then fit a fermentation lock and leave until all fermentation has ceased.

LOGANBERRY WINES

For sweet wine
2 lb loganberries · 1 lb raisins · 2½ lb sugar · yeast
nutrient · water as in method

For dry wine
2½ lb loganberries · 2–2¼ lb sugar · yeast
nutrient · water as in method

Crush the loganberries by hand, put them in a fermenting vessel with chopped raisins (if being used), and pour on 4 pints of water. Crush and dissolve 1 Campden tablet in a little warm water and stir this into the mixture. Leave for an hour or so. Meanwhile, boil half the sugar to be used in 2 pints of water for 2 minutes and, when cool, add to the mixture, giving it a thorough stirring.

Add yeast and nutrient and ferment in a warm place for 7 to 8 days, stirring daily. After this time, strain out the solids and return the strained wine to the (cleaned) fermenting vessel. Boil the remaining sugar in 1 pint of water for 2 minutes and, when cool, add to the rest. Leave to ferment for a further 3 to 4 days. Then pour into a jar, fit a fermentation lock, and leave until all fermentation has ceased.

REDCURRANT WINES

For dry wine
$2\frac{1}{2}$ lb redcurrents · $2\frac{1}{2}$ lb sugar · yeast · nutrient water as in method

For sweet wine
$2\frac{1}{2}$ lb redcurrents · 1 lb tin strawberries · $2\frac{1}{2}$ lb sugar (less sugar than normal because of the syrup from the strawberries) · yeast · nutrient · approx. 1 gallon water as in method

Remove the stalks from the currants, put them in a fermenting vessel, and crush well by hand. Pour on 4 pints of water. Crush and dissolve 1 Campden tablet in a little warm water and stir this into the mixture. Leave for an hour or so. Meanwhile, boil half the sugar in 2 pints water for 2 minutes and,

when cool, add to the mixture, giving it a thorough
stirring.

Add the tinned strawberries (if being used) and
then the yeast and nutrient. Ferment in a warm
place for 6 to 7 days. After this time, strain out the
solids and press as much as possible. Return the
strained wine to the (cleaned) fermenting vessel.
Boil the remaining sugar in 2 pints of water for 2
minutes and, when cool, add to the rest.

Leave to ferment for further 3 to 4 days. Then
pour carefully into a jar. Fit a fermentation lock,
and leave until all fermentation has ceased.

DAMSON WINES

Damsons make a delightful table wine as well as a
dessert wine. The addition of prunes improves the
dessert type.

Table wine
    5 lb damsons · 2½ lb sugar · yeast · nutrient
            water as in method

Dessert wine
    4 lb damsons · 1 lb prunes · 3 lb sugar · yeast
        nutrient · water as in method

Remove the stalks of the damsons, and rinse the
fruit under the tap if it is at all dusty. Crush as
much as possible but do not expect much juice as
this fruit gives very little. Pour on 4 pints of water.
Crush and dissolve 1 Campden tablet in a little
warm water and stir this into the mixture. Leave for
a few hours. Meanwhile, boil half the sugar to be
used in 2 pints of water for 2 minutes and, when

cool, stir into the mixture, giving it a thorough churning.

Add the yeast and nutrient (and dried prunes if being used), and ferment in a warm place for 7 to 8 days, stirring daily and crushing prunes by hand.

After this time, strain out the solids and return the strained wine to the (cleaned) fermenting vessel. Allow to ferment for a further 3 to 4 days. Then transfer to a jar, leaving as much deposit behind as you can. Boil the remaining sugar in 1 pint of water for 2 minutes and when cool add to the jar. Then fit a fermentation lock and leave until all fermentation has ceased.

PLUM WINES

I have found that plums can be made into several wine types, all of which are excellent. The following three recipes make distinctly different types. Black plums give best results.

Table wine
> 3 lb plums · 2½ lb sugar · yeast · nutrient
> water as in method

Dessert wine
> 4–5 lb plums · 3 lb sugar · yeast · nutrient
> water as in method

Port-style
> 4 lb plums · 2 lb elderberries · yeast · nutrient
> water as in method

Remove the stalks from the plums, and rinse the fruit under the tap if it is at all dusty. Put it in a fermenting vessel and crush well by hand. If elder-berries are being used, strip them from the stalks, crush by hand, and put them with the plums. Pour on 4 pints of water and mix well. Crush and dis-solve 1 Campden tablet in a little warm water and stir this into the mixture. Leave for a few hours. Meanwhile, boil half the sugar to be used in 2 pints of water for 2 minutes and, when cool, stir into the mixture.

Add the yeast and nutrient and ferment for 7 to 8 days. After this time, strain out the solids and return the strained wine to the (cleaned) fermenting vessel. Leave to ferment for a further 3 to 4 days. Then pour carefully into a jar, leaving as much deposit behind as you can. Boil the remaining sugar in 1 pint of water for 2 minutes and, when cool, add to the jar. Then fit a fermentation lock and leave until all fermentation has ceased.

Wines from Concentrated Grape Juice

Very little need be said on the subject of making wines from concentrated grape juices because the main feature is to dilute the juice to a suitable specific gravity and then to ferment it. Careful study of the hydrometer section, especially the chart on page 69 showing how to dilute the juice, will show you exactly what to do and how to do it.

Having obtained the required specific gravity, you merely add yeast and nutrient – very often sup-plied with the concentrate – and then ferment it in a fermenting vessel for 8 to 10 days or until fermentation slows down. After this time, you put the wine into jars free of as much deposit as possible and make any sugar addition required. The actual timing of sugar additions is a matter entirely for yourself to decide.

A trial quart of concentrate will make one gallon of top-class wine at a cost of about 14s. This works out at less than two shillings a bottle. Having used a trial quart, you will find it a lot cheaper to buy by the gallon, but a trial quart is worthwhile in order to obtain experience. Afterwards you may proceed with greater confidence. Bear in mind that when you have a gallon of concentrate you are able to make several varieties of wines. You can make two gallons of sweet and two gallons of dry, or a gallon each of sweet, medium, and dry and still have enough left to make an extra gallon of any one.

There is quite a variety of concentrates to choose from. All make top-class wines, but naturally, each differs from the next according to its country of origin. Concentrates available from the various suppliers listed at the end of this book come from Spain, France, Cyprus, and (I believe) Algeria.

A fermentation lock is used here as with other wines. So when the wine is put into the jar from the fermentation vessel, a fermentation lock is fitted for the duration of fermentation. When fermentation has ceased, the wine is treated in exactly the same way as other wines.

Whenever the subject of concentrated grape juice crops up, I am always asked which I consider the best. And I always reply that it is a matter of what you want. Each grape juice makes a different type of wine. Each wine varies, although it has the basic flavour of the grapes used. On top of this, we ourselves can make variations by using different yeasts and different amounts of sugar to produce varying wine types.

I am also often asked if using grape concentrate would be a better way of making Vermouth when using T'Noirot extracts, or for making Dubonnet with the addition of cinchona essence. There is no doubt that using grape juice would be a little better, but using this in conjunction with T'Noirot extracts would be expensive and the overall result not all that much better. The same applies to making Dubonnet. If this can be made with less expensive materials, then it is common sense to use them.

Grape concentrates should, in my view, be used alone for the very simple reason that they make top-class wines without additions. Some people use less grape juice with a little other fruit or dried fruit to obtain special results or to make the concentrate go a lot further. However, I cannot go into this here as I have given many recipes and covered this aspect of wine-making fully in 'Home Wine-making all the Year Round'.

A number of readers are sure to want to know just what a concentrated grape juice is, so let me explain. Concentrated grape juice is the pure juice of grapes with the natural water content removed. This is usually achieved by what is known as the vacuum process. The main object is to reduce the bulk in order to transport it in much less space and at the same time produce so high a sugar content that it will not ferment in storage or in transit. The grape concentrates you receive are therefore pure and free from preservatives. When we add water to dilute the concentrate we merely make good the amount taken out at the start. We produce, as near as possible, a grape juice in the same condition as it was before it was concentrated, minus the pips and skins.

IMITATION HOCK

Here is a recipe given me by a member of the Orpington Circle. The wine made with this really did taste top-rate. I have made one slight modification. Forgive me, Orpington.

1 lb raisins · 3 lb sugar · juice of 2 lemons and
3 oranges · ½ lb potatoes · yeast · nutrient
approx. 1 gallon water

Chop the raisins and put them in a fermenting vessel. Peel the potatoes thinly and boil them gently for 15 minutes or until the water becomes clear. Strain onto the raisins and allow the mixture to cool well. Add the juice of the oranges and lemons. Then add yeast and nutrient and ferment for 10 days, stirring daily.

After this time, strain out the solids and return the strained wine to the (cleaned) fermenting vessel. Boil the sugar in 2 pints of water for 2 minutes and, when cool, add to the rest. Leave to ferment for a further 7 to 8 days. Then pour into a jar, fit a fermentation lock, and leave until all fermentation has ceased.

Wines Using More Modern Ingredients

The heading may not describe precisely the nature of ingredients used in this section. But it shows that, while hedgerow and garden fruits will always be the main standby of the majority of wine-makers, there is a noticeable swing towards ingredients which are obtainable ready-packed from home wine-making suppliers. In my book 'Home Wine-making all the Year Round,' I covered the making of wines from many readily obtainable ingredients very fully, giving a great variety of recipes and methods for using often unheard-of ingredients. There is not space here to cover such ground again – indeed, it would not be wise to do so. Nevertheless, I am able to give a variety of recipes that have been evolved since the other book was published.

IMITATION TOKAY

Although I have not made this myself, I know a number of people who make an excellent imitation of Tokay with this recipe.

8 oz rosehip shells · $\frac{1}{4}$ lb raisins · 4 oz dried figs juice of 2 lemons and 2 oranges · $\frac{1}{4}$ pint freshly made strong tea · $2\frac{3}{4}$ lb sugar · yeast · nutrient approx. 1 gallon water

Chop finely or mince the raisins and figs and put them in a fermenting vessel. Pour on 4 pints of cool, boiled water. Meanwhile, wash the rosehip shells thoroughly, put these with the fruit, and add a further 1 pint of cool, boiled water.

Crush and dissolve 1 Campden tablet in a little warm water and stir this into the mixture. Leave covered for a few hours. Meanwhile, boil half the sugar to be used in 2 pints of water for 2 minutes and, when cool, mix it well with the ingredients. Give the mixture a thorough stirring, and add the tea, the strained juice of the oranges and lemons, and then the yeast and nutrient.

Cover and ferment in a warm place for 8 to 9 days, stirring daily. After this, strain out the solids and wring out as dry as possible. Return the strained wine to the (cleaned) fermenting vessel. Boil the remaining sugar in 1 pint of water for 2 minutes and, when cool, add to the rest.

Allow the must to ferment for a further 2 to 3 days, or a little longer if fermentation is vigorous. When fermentation has slowed down a little, pour carefully into a jar. Then fit a fermentation lock and leave until all fermentation has ceased.

CLARET

For those who like a light and really dry claret, this recipe should prove a boon. This wine may be drunk while quite young — say, six months after fermentation has ceased.

$\frac{1}{2}$ lb dried elderberries · 3 bananas · juice
2 lemons · 2 lb sugar · yeast · nutrient
approx. 1 gallon water

Thoroughly wash the elderberries in several lots of water. Put them in a fermenting vessel with 6 pints of cool, boiled water. Crush and dissolve 1 Campden tablet in a little warm water and stir this into the mixture. Allow to stand for 12 hours.

Boil all the sugar to be used in 1 pint of water for 2 minutes. When cool, pour onto the fruit and stir thoroughly. Add the lemon juice (strained), peeled and crushed bananas, yeast and nutrient. Cover and leave to ferment for 5 to 6 days.

After this time, strain out the solids and wring as dry as possible. Return the strained wine to the (cleaned) fermenting vessel and leave to ferment for a further 3 to 4 days. Then pour into a jar, fit a fermentation lock, and leave until all fermentation has ceased.

Only lovers of very dry wines should make this wine. True, it could be sweetened if too dry, but this would give rise to renewed fermentation because of the rather lower-than-average alcohol content. In any case bone-dry wines are usually better for being lower in alcohol than the sweeter sorts. So, on the whole, it is best to make this wine for what it is and leave it at that.

BILBERRY WINES FROM DRIED FRUITS

Dried bilberries make two excellent wines, the claret being very different to the type made with dried elderberries. The dessert wine which is sweeter, needs to be kept a little longer to be at its best, but the dry wine may be used quite young.

Dry Bilberry Wine
$\frac{3}{4}$ lb dried bilberries · juice 3 lemons · $2\frac{1}{4}$ lb
sugar · yeast · nutrient
water as in method

Dessert Bilberry Wine

   1 lb dried bilberries · 1 lb raisins · juice 3
lemons · 2½ lb sugar (up to 3 lb for sweeter
      wine) · yeast · nutrient
       water as in method

Wash the bilberries thoroughly under a fast-running tap as they are usually very dusty when received. Soak in 2 pints of water in which half a Campden tablet has been dissolved until they soak it up. Add a little more water if necessary. Keep well covered during this time. Do not discard this water.

Boil half the sugar to be used in 4 pints of water for 2 minutes and, when cool, mix with the fruit. Add the chopped raisins (if these are being used) and the strained juice of three lemons. Add yeast and nutrient, cover, and ferment in a warm place for 7 to 8 days, stirring daily. Then strain out the solids and wring as dry as you can.

Return the strained wine to the (cleaned) fermenting vessel and ferment for a further 3 to 4 days. Then pour carefully into a jar leaving as much deposit behind as you can. Boil the remaining sugar in 1 pint of water for 2 minutes and, when cool, add to the jar. Then fit a fermentation lock and leave until all fermentation has ceased.

APRICOT WINES
FROM DRIED FRUITS

Dried apricots make several very good wines when used in conjunction with other ingredients. The two recipes given here make first-rate wines of considerable character. The sweet one may be made into an excellent imitation of the very popular apricot liqueur by adding up to 3 fl oz of Vodka per bottle or into quite a good apricot brandy by adding 2 to 2½ fl oz of brandy per bottle. The spirits should be added only when the wines are finished products ready for use. Wines so treated may be kept for as long as you wish.

It may be necessary to sweeten the sweet wine to be made into a liqueur owing to the dilution of the sweetness by the added spirit. If sweetening is necessary, put a little of the wine to be treated into a polythene or china jug with one or two teaspoonfuls of sugar. Stand the jug in a saucepan with a little water in it and bring the water nearly to the boil. Stir the wine until the sugar is dissolved, and let it cool. Then pour the spirit into a bottle and add the sweetened wine.

Dry Apricot Wine
    1 lb dried apricots · juice 1 lemon · ¼ pint freshly made strong tea · 1 lb sultanas · 2 lb
                sugar · yeast · nutrient
                water as in method

Sweet Apricot Wine
    1 lb dried apricots · juice 1 lemon · ¼ pint freshly made strong tea · 1 lb raisins · 3 lb
                sugar · yeast · nutrient
                water as in method

Wash the apricots well unless pre-packed in polythene. Soak them overnight in 2 pints of water. This water will form part of the overall amount used. Cut up the fruits quite small and put them in a fermenting vessel with the chopped raisins.

Boil half the sugar to be used in 4 pints of water for 2 minutes and pour over the fruit. Add strained tea and allow the mixture to cool.

Then add strained lemon juice, yeast and nutrient. Cover and leave in a warm place to ferment for 7 to 8 days, stirring daily. Then strain out the solids and return the strained wine to the (cleaned) fermenting vessel.

Boil the remaining sugar in 1 pint of water for 2 minutes and, when cool, add to the rest. Ferment for a further 3 to 4 days. Then pour carefully into a jar, fit a fermentation lock, and leave until all fermentation has ceased.

Recipes for Beers

I do not intend to give a large variety of recipes here. For one thing, there is no room. For another, there is a very large range in my book 'Home Brewing without Failures'.

These recipes are simple and straightforward and are intended to initiate readers into making beers, rather than give them adventurous recipes that they might find difficult to use and which, owing to their inexperience, might not result in the sort of beer they are aiming at.

I do not claim that these recipes cannot be improved upon – all recipes can. But they are for those who want to gain experience in order to give them confidence to try more elaborate recipes and methods.

When evolving recipes, we tend to use rather more ingredients than are necessary. This applies not only to wines but also to beers. We all do it and, for the life of me, I cannot imagine why — unless it is because we are afraid of using too little of each of certain ingredients.

This is not to say that earlier recipes will not make good beers, because they certainly will. But it often turns out that we get quite as good results with less ingredients. I do not mean less in number, but less in weight. For this reason, you will find that the following recipes contain smaller amounts of ingredients than most other recipes.

BRAVERY'S STOUT

1 lb caramelized dried malt extract · 1 lb dried light malt extract · 2 lb demerara sugar · 3 oz hops · 1 tablespoon black treacle · ½ teaspoon citric acid · 1 teaspoon salt · yeast · nutrient water as in method

Put the hops in a muslin bag with something like a glass marble to keep them submerged. Boil in a saucepan with 2 pints of water for about 15 minutes, with the lid on. Take out the bag, squeeze well, and pour the hop water into a fermenting vessel.

Add the malts, treacle, salt and citric acid, and make up to 2 gallons with boiling water. Stir well, cover, and allow to cool to about 65° to 70°F. Then add yeast and nutrient and ferment in a warm place for 7 to 8 days.

If you are making draught stout that will contain no gas, merely allow the beer to ferment until it goes 'flat' in appearance or until you are sure fermentation has ceased. Then siphon into screw-top bottles. If you are making gaseous beer and using a hydrometer, take frequent readings until 1·005 is reached and then siphon into bottles.

If you are making gaseous beer without a hydrometer, allow the beer to ferment out. Take a little of the beer, warm it gently, and dissolve in it $2\frac{1}{4}$ oz sugar for each gallon you are making. Stir this into the bulk. Allow the yeast to settle again – four hours is long enough – and siphon into screw-top bottles.

LIGHT MILD ALE

2 lb light dried malt extract · $\frac{1}{2}$ lb caramelized malt extract · $1\frac{1}{2}$ lb white sugar · 2 oz hops $\frac{1}{2}$ teaspoon citric acid · $\frac{1}{2}$ teaspoon salt · yeast nutrient · water as in method

Follow exactly the method for 'Bravery's Stout'.

BEST BITTER

2 lb light dried malt extract · $1\frac{1}{2}$ lb white sugar 4 oz hops · 2 pints tea made with 4 teaspoons tea · $\frac{1}{2}$ teaspoon citric acid · $\frac{1}{2}$ teaspoon salt yeast · nutrient · water as in method

Follow exactly the method for 'Bravery's Stout', adding the strained tea before pouring boiling water onto the ingredients.

LIGHT ALE

2 lb pale dried malt extract · $\frac{1}{2}$ lb golden syrup
1$\frac{1}{2}$ lb sugar · 2$\frac{1}{2}$ oz hops · $\frac{1}{2}$ teaspoon citric acid
$\frac{1}{2}$ teaspoon salt · yeast · nutrient
water as in method

Follow exactly the method for 'Bravery's Stout'.

BROWN ALE

2 lb dark malt extract · $\frac{1}{2}$ lb caramelized malt
extract · 1$\frac{1}{2}$ lb demerara sugar · 2 oz hops
$\frac{1}{2}$ teaspoon citric acid · $\frac{1}{2}$ teaspoon salt · 1 tablespoon black treacle · yeast · nutrient
water as in method

Follow exactly the method for 'Bravery's Stout',
adding the treacle before pouring the boiling water
over the ingredients.

The Drake Trial Tube

At a time when this book was in an advanced stage of production, the Drake Trial Tube was brought to my notice.

I decided at once that this is just the thing for my readers because it simplifies taking gravities. It does away with the need to pour wine into a trial flask and therefore minimises the risk of bacterial infection and also prevents wines and their deposits being disturbed.

I consider this to be a great advance and I am sure my readers will be quick to see the advantages. However, this was brought to my notice too late to include it in the Hydrometer Chapter and too late to cancel expensive art work already commissioned. I therefore decided to leave the hydrometer chapter as it stands together with the illustrations and to include details of the Drake Trial Tube as a separate piece.

The illustrations speak for themselves. It costs no more than an ordinary hydrometer and its trial jar. Sole distributors are: Rogers Meads Ltd., 27 Vicarage Road, Wednesfield, Staffs.

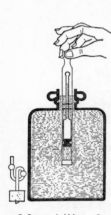

1 Remove bubbler. Insert tube till hydrometer just floats.

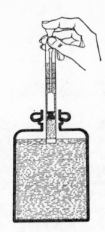

2 Apply finger, lift tube & read hydrometer. Keep bottom of the tube below the liquid in the vessel.

3 Lower with finger in place. Remove finger lift tube and drain.

4 Rinse under tap. Never use hot water, this would loosen the plastic.

5 Replace bubbler.

6 Return to vase of bisulphite (Campden) solution ready for next trial.

166

Appendix

SUPPLIERS OF HOME WINE-MAKING EQUIPMENT

United Kingdom

Brew it Yourself Ltd., 135/6 Upper Street, London, N.1.

W. A. E. Busby Ltd., 96 Farringdon Road, London, E.C.1.

Joseph Bryant Ltd., 95 Old Market Street, Bristol 2.

Maurice D. Chant, 519 Fishponds Road, Fishponds, Bristol.

Handicrafts & Utilities (Southampton) Ltd., 42/3 St. Mary Street, Southampton.

Hoyle's Home Wine Supplies, 131/3 Main Street, Auchinleck, Ayrshire.

Joly & Bradburn Ltd., The Broadway, Drayton, Portsmouth, Hants; The Precinct, Waterlooville, Hants.

Leigh-Williams & Sons, Tattenhall, Nr. Chester (Wholesalers).

W. R. Loftus, 1-3 Charlotte Street, London, W.1; 12-16 The Terrace, Fleet Street, Torquay (Postal orders).

Riverside Home Wine Equipment, Dept. F/1, 130 Bridge Lane, Frodsham, Warrington, Lancs.

Semplex Home Brews Ltd., Old Hall Works, Struart Road, Higher Tranmere, Birkenhead.

Southern Vineyards, 36 Conway Street, Hove, Sussex.

A. & B. Temple, 62/4 High Street, Newton-Le-Willows, Lancs.

Vina Home Winemaking Supplies, 88 College Road, Crosby, Liverpool.

Vinaide, 28/28a Swan Street, Manchester 4.

Winemakers Equipment Ltd., 242 Deansgate, Manchester 3.

Canada

The Amateur Wine Shop, Catalog Dept. G, P.O. Box 35, Verdun, Que.

Messrs. Semplex of Canada, Box 3092, Station 'C', Ottawa, Ontaria.

APPENDIX

New Zealand
Brewers Trading Co., P.O. Box 593, Christchurch.

U.S.A.
Aetna Bottle Co. Inc., 708 Rainier Avenue South, Seattle 44, Washington.
Semplex of U.S.A., Box 7208, Minneapolis, Minnesota 55412.